The Concise Guide to Car Numbers

THE CONCISE GUIDE TO CAR NUMBERS

TONY HILL

Acknowledgements

Steve Wood, David Parr, Matthew Bowler, Mike Barnshaw, Martin Hill, Colin Cowperthwaite, John Harrison, Paul Rawden (USA), Hannah Mindham, Winifred Rule, Steve Conner, Chris Money, David Kempson, Frederick Wackett, Mike Derrick, Paul Milsom, Safer Motoring, Hunts County News, Daily Mirror, Western Mail & Echo. Plus all other contributors too numerous to mention but equally worthy of grateful thanks.

First edition 1982
Second edition 1983

Published by; CAR NUMBERS MONTHLY
P.O. BOX 1, BRADFORD-ON-AVON, WILTSHIRE, BA15 1YQ
Tel: (0225) 782640
ISBN 0-9508266-1-8

Printed in Great Britain by
F.A. Slugg & Co. Ltd., Trowbridge, Wiltshire.
Design and artwork by Annette Habershon.

Cover, and all colour photographs by Martin Hill.

FRONT COVER: The author with his Rolls-Royce and number plate MAD 1.

BACK COVER: Panther Lima (JJJ 55) and Porsche 911 SC (9200 LJ) belonging to Leslie Jones of Reigate, Surrey.

Introduction

To maintain a concise guide to car numbers, I have had to keep pace with the bureaucrats at DVLC, Swansea, as they change the transfer rules and so alter the whole numbers game. Of course they claim that the Government make the changes, however, as you read through the various sections of this book, you'll no doubt get the impression that the Government haven't a clue and are merely puppets to the DVLC dictatorship.

The Government are keen to reap a multi-million pounds profit from the numbers game, but they are reluctant to ease up on their bureaucracy. In 1981 Norman Fowler, Secretary of State for Transport said in a Consultation Paper that the public have been subjected to a "tortuous set of transfer rules", He implied that those days were over, however, in July 1983, the public are still subjected to virtually the same tortuous rules and in September 1983, approximately forty categories of vehicles are to be excluded from the cherished transfer scheme. Whilst admittedly, it is marginally easier to carry out a transfer these days, I believe that a "Concise Guide to Car Numbers" is an essential work of reference for the baffled motorist who simply wishes to transfer a registration number from one vehicle to another. I hope this guide will prove informative and entertaining.

Pictured below: DVLC, Swansea. (The Driver and Vehicle Licensing Centre at Morriston Swansea). The nerve centre of the car numbers game.

My Life of Car Numbers

I started in business, whilst I was still at school. My only transport was a Dawes Dapper bicycle and the assets of the business amounted to a bucket and a second hand chamois leather. I traded as C. W. A. H. (Car Washing At Home). It was all a far cry from the hassle of running one of the country's leading car number plate businesses. There were no Civil Servants to dictate the policies of operation. The only problems were the weather and punctures.

I built up quite a successful round and made enough money to buy plenty of records and to see the leading pop groups each Monday night, and still manage to save. I remember one of my regular customers telling me, one freezing afternoon, that I would run a big business when I was older. She was so impressed with the way I was running the car washing enterprise. It could have been that comment that prompted me to try. However, I cannot say that I am exactly in the "big business" league. I don't think I ever will be and neither do I wish to be. I can't really see the point in spending so much time and effort building up a massive business empire at the cost of sacrificing leisure time.

A typical day for me, starts with getting up at 8.30 am and soaking in a hot bath until 9.30 or 10.00, depending on how many newspapers there are to read. It isn't a total waste of time. I find it most useful to plan the day ahead, and I certainly couldn't do that, once I am sat behind my office desk. If you thought Piccadilly Circus was busy, let me assure you, just looking into my office would drive you dizzy. My morning bath is absolutely essential, besides, I have my breakfast in there as well. There's many a time that I don't even have a wash when I'm in the bath. It may not be a conventional start to the day, but there again I am not exactly a conventional person. I couldn't run the car numbers business, if I was.

The rest of the day is spent opening mail, planning advertising campaigns, writing articles for Car Numbers Monthly, keeping an eye on my staff and attending to semi-business interests such as my record company. Throughout the day I am plagued with people trying to sell me car numbers. That's one of the hazards of running massive advertising campaigns in the national press. I work some evenings, when I'm not playing tennis or weight lifting. Fortunately, I have a very hard working and understanding staff; Doreen, Helen, Mary, and Bet. I reward them with adequate pay and evenings out on the town. I can assure you, that running a car numbers business can easily drive you crazy, you just have to unwind or you would end up in a loony bin. Although dealing with the Civil Servants at Swansea is a permanent nightmare and the problems of maintaining a successful business are sometimes traumatic, I am not complaining. The problems are so varied, it's the spice of life!

Just how did I get involved in this jungle of bureaucracy and high finance? I am not an intellectual and I didn't even study commerce or business at school. When I took my eight 'O' levels at the end of my fifth year at St. Brendan's College in Bristol and failed the lot (it was unheard of at such a good school), they accepted me back for a repeat fifth year and at the end of that I failed all eight exams yet again. My business success can only be summed up, as luck.

Having tried ventures varying between landscape gardening and office work, within only a few years of leaving school, I had the luckiest break of my life. A car was advertised in The Sunday Times, it was a 1946 Morris Ten, in original condition, complete with MOT and tax and in perfect running order, the cost being £200 to include the registration number HTV 1. I thought it was the bargain of 1973. I knew nothing about personalised car registrations, but I was aware that HTV, my local independent television company, were bound to be interested, in it. I concluded the deal that same day, with the vendor, a London car dealer, and drove the car back to Wiltshire there and then. I just couldn't believe my luck. The car itself was a real

1

collector's item and it went like a dream. I drove it everywhere for a month, until the novelty wore off. Then came the second stroke of luck, another car was advertised in The Sunday Times. It was a 1960 Rover 100, with the registration number 1 HTV. I just HAD to buy it and once again secured the deal the same day at £200 and drove the car back from Cardiff to Wiltshire.

The next day I offered the pair of registrations to H.T.V. Ltd. To my horror, they were not interested. Furthermore, Lord Harlech, the Chairman had reputedly issued instructions to his staff, not to buy either of the number plates. This may or may not have been true but the fact was, that I was now the owner of a pair of registration numbers, that had no relevance to my name. I didn't want to sell the numbers, so I thought of creating a stage name for my showbiz career (I had spent three weeks in a play with the Bristol Old Vic Company), so I called myself Howard T. Vernon. The story made a splash in the local papers and as a result, someone phoned me, saying that there was already a film star called Howard Vernon. That was typical of my luck of all the combinations of names available to me, I had to choose that one! I immediately gave the idea up and put both of the cars up for sale in The Sunday Times. I had sold the pair within a matter of days and made £200 profit on the deal. The owner, not being short of a bob or two, let me keep the two old cars, provided that I arranged the transfer of the numbers to two of his own cars. I went to the Local Taxation Office, to find out how to transfer the numbers. It was all quite painless and within a matter of days the entire transaction was completed.

I had accidentally started a car numbers business. It may never have happened if the purchaser of HTV 1 and 1 HTV had just acquired the cars from me, or if HTV Ltd. had purchased the pair in the first place. I had discovered that it was easy to buy, sell and transfer registration marks.

The next number I purchased was CCP 20 on a 98cc 1951 Bown, Autocycle. It was a real boneshaker, but it was in good working order. I advertised it in The Sunday Times and also stated "numbers wanted" in the advertisement. I bought two or three numbers, as a result, but didn't sell CCP 20. The other numbers didn't sell either, after a few weeks of advertising and this coupled with the bill from The Sunday Times, left me penniless. I had to look for a job to raise cash.

Craftily, I looked for a driving job. I needed something to keep me on the road and maybe pick up a number plate bargain. I couldn't get a job locally and ended up as a van driver for a firm of photographic suppliers in Bristol. The problem was, that the only roadworthy vehicle I had, was the old motorcycle. I drove that to work every day until the firm felt sorry for me and let me use the van for commuting. It was such good fun, that I kept the job for six months. At the same time I was buying and selling a few numbers. I may have kept the job longer, if I hadn't taken an extended holiday, camping on the Cote d'Azur. I blew every penny I had, in and around St. Tropez and when I got back to England, I had to start looking for another job. I managed to get another delivery job and after working for a month I was offered a motorcycle with an interesting plate, although I can't remember the number, it made me enough money to quit the delivery round and buy a few more vehicles with distinctive numbers.

One night at a village dance, a chap introduced himself, as "Pop", he said he knew that I bought vehicles with distinctive registrations and he had one that may interest me, PAM 1. It was on a motorcycle and he could take me to see it the next day. I couldn't believe my luck. The next day I frantically phoned around the leading dealers. I had been dealing with the likes of Davis Numbers and John Gifford ("Yours Personally"), for several months. They were talking in terms of £1,000 for PAM 1. It gave me plenty of scope for negotiation with Pop. Then came the bad news, Pop, got in touch and said that he had made a mistake, the number plate was PAM 95 and not PAM 1. Although it was a bitter disappointment, it heralded the start of a long association with the irrepressible Pop. The first deal we had was PAM 95. I paid him £50 for it, of which £40 was clear profit. He was delighted and set out to find more numbers.

Pop was always keen to buy and sell numbers and he didn't really take a great interest in motoring laws. If he found a car or motorcycle for sale, he would drive it home without MOT, tax or insurance. He was only interested in money. He was also a crazy driver, he would drive at excessive speeds, without a care in the world. I dreaded travelling with him, but often it was essential, to clinch a deal. As the money came his way, the crazier he got. He acquired a taste for old Jaguars. He bought every old heap he could find and literally ran each one into the ground. It would be no exaggeration to say that he got through one Jaguar a week. At first, they were all pre-1963 cars, that had interesting numbers. I bought the plate and he exterminated the car. Then things got worse and he started buying post 1965 Mark 10 Jaguars. It was as if they were two a penny and available on every street corner. Pop was magnetised. One day, I had the misfortune of helping him collect a car. He was using his pride and joy, 999 BAM, an exceptionally good 2.4, to tow a battered old car trailer . We were almost home, when a wheel came off the trailer, we stopped, as the wheel overtook us and disappeared around a corner.

Business was beginning to boom, as Pop found more and more numbers. This created a problem, Pop had been using some parking spaces on his housing estate to store all these vehicles and to cut the rubbish up for scrap metal. Not surprisingly the residents became a little fed up with him burning the midnight oil, in more senses than one. The whole thing had got out of hand. He even used to smash a car up with a sledge hammer if it wouldn't start. I saw at least two being "put to sleep". Then came a lucky break. He befriended another loopy driver whose father owned a smallholding. He was allowed to use about ¼ acre, in return for tidying the whole place up. However, as I was buying most of the cars Pop took to the smallholding, the agreement with the owner, Mr. Shepherd, seemed to disintegrate. I ended up having to pay Mr. Shepherd a weekly rental for storage. There was little choice, I had at least thirty cars there myself and Pop was busily piling up scrap metal from the cars he was cutting up and smashing up. The Shepherds' kept chickens there as well, but as time progressed, so the stock decreased, it may have been foxy Pop with his sledgehammer or the chickens didn't like living in a scrap yard. As for tidying the place up, the view from the Shepherds' kitchen window became more and more depressing. Eventually, Mr. Shepherd "blew a fuse". However, I managed to calm him down by offering his wife a job as a part time secretary. We used their phone number for advertising in The Sunday Times and I started regular advertising, trading as Elite Registrations.

Pop progressed from Jaguars to Dodge Pick Up Trucks (left hand drive monsters) after 999 BAM came to rest. The sad day started with Pop and some of his fans, joy riding and getting into a spot of bother with the Police. During a high speed chase, the Jaguar mounted the pavement and jumped over a garden wall, demolishing part of it and finishing up on a poor fellow's prize vegetable patch. They lost the pursuing Police car but were then confronted by the irate gardener. Pop agreed to pay for the damage and repair the wall himself.

As business continued to boom, Pop began to resent my success. He could see my advertisements in The Sunday Times, showing most of the numbers that he had sold to me at considerably lower prices. His indignation was not justified, although it was impossible to explain to him, that the cost of advertising was astronomical. I tried my best to get Pop set up in his own numbers business, I even offered to get a telephone installed in his house. It was to no avail. He was too busy having a great time, treating the roads of Trowbridge as a banger racing circuit.

I called at the smallholding one day and found Pop smashing up several of my cars with a JCB that he had borrowed from a building site. It wasn't the first time that he smashed up my cars. I also knew that he had been syphoning my petrol and permanently borrowing odds and ends. The smallholding was in a disgraceful state, I felt really sorry for Mr. Shepherd. However, that was breaking point for him and he ordered Pop off the land. Even after this, whole cars were disappearing from the smallholding, so I decided enough was enough and started looking for other storage space as far away from Pop as possible.

I should explain that although Pop had been ripping me off all that time, I didn't really mind. I just treated it as a business expense. After all, condition of the vehicle was immaterial to qualify for transfer and in many cases the vehicles were not even inspected. I knew that Pop was getting a great deal of satisfaction every time he delivered a blow to one of my vehicles, so I was happy that he was happy.

Pop continued in business, by taking old cars straight to scrap yards. He used one of his newly acquired Dodge trucks. There were no number plates on the vehicle, in fact the only thing that was legal, was one of the tyres. He managed to steer clear of the Police for an extraordinarily long period, until one day his luck ran out as he crashed into a ten feet high wall, demolishing most of it and unable to drive out of the debris. The Police were quickly on the scene and Pop was charged with 39 motoring offences.

During the few months that Pop was waiting for his court case to come up, he kept selling me numbers that he found, and doing odd jobs. One day he took a car plus trailer and his brother. "Bubbles", to collect a car (PAD 555, I believe). I went along with them to sort out the cash side of the transaction. Between the three of us we managed to get the old car on the trailer but as we made our way home it was obvious that the car we were using to tow the trailer with, didn't have enough power to cope. Apart from that, Pop hadn't secured the old car on the trailer properly and as we approached a very steep hill, Pop had an inspired thought. He told Bubbles to sit in the old car on the trailer and keep his foot on the brake, to stop it rolling off the trailer. It didn't work at all, because, as we carried on up the hill, I could see Bubbles frantically depressing the brake to no avail and as the whole rig got slower and slower, Pop calmly told me that there were defective brakes on the car we were driving. As we travelled at snails' pace, I could see Bubbles and the old car getting closer and closer to the back of the trailer. I had a vision of us all careering back to the bottom of the hill. However, Pop with luck on his side again, got to the top. We stopped to let Bubbles out and discovered that the old car was only an inch away from the end of the trailer. It was still liable to fall off on the rest of the journey home. I suggested that we push the car back on the trailer, but Pop said he had another idea, and one just did not argue with him. To my amazement he turned the rig in the middle of the road (a fairly busy "B" road), and calmly reversed the trailer into a wall and so pushed the old car back on the trailer. I am sure that it will be a sight that all the other motorists who witnessed the episode will never forget.

Pop and I went to the car numbers rally at Beaulieu that year. Pop managed to convince the man on the gate, that he was a member of the dealers' Association and we got in for nothing. It was quite interesting to put faces to the names of the dealers as they picnicked next to their expensive motor cars. I thought to myself that I would be joining the dealer ranks at the next rally if I worked hard enough. It was a thought that materialised.

The last time I had a deal with Pop, was just before his court case was due, when I sold him a Triumph. It was a good reliable car and I sold it for a "song". Unfortunately, he was banned for three years, the following day, (or perhaps I ought to say, "fortunately", for other motorists). He employed his brother as a chauffeur and he even paid to have the car taxed! However, the car only lasted a few weeks. His brother wrote it off, doing a "Dukes of Hazard" over a canal bridge.

Despite all the ups and downs with Pop, I will always be grateful for the help he gave me and shall never forget that most likeable of rogues.

Shortly after Pop faded out of the scene, I met a cheerful lady at a concert. Her name was Cara Boniface. We started chatting and although I was only able to get the odd word in between her continuous talking, when she paused for breath, I established that she lived with her husband at a farm near Bradford on Avon. They didn't work the farm, so I asked what chances there were of using some of the land for storage of old vehicles. She had a word with her husband, Frank, and he permitted me to use an empty barn and surrounding area. He even let me use a caravan as an office. Although cramped for space, it served the purpose. A few weeks later Frank could see that I was seriously involved in the business and let me use a room in the farmhouse, to set up a proper office. That chance meeting at the concert, with Cara, was to establish my business, although, I didn't realise it at the time.

By the middle of 1975, I was firmly established with the Boniface family at the farm. I even employed Cara as a secretary and I also employed a driver/clerk, Andrew Stevens, to help with the rapidly expanding business. I applied to join the dealers' Association (then known as the PNDA) and was invited to attend a meeting in London. I didn't really know how I would be treated, after all, I was comfortably the youngest of the membership. I remember putting on a voice to try to impress them as I told the packed room, why I wanted to become a member (it was the sort of voice, most people use when trying to impress someone on the telephone). I must have looked and sounded a right wally. However, the meeting was action packed, with plenty of useful information.

In the summer of 1976, I went on holiday to St. Tropez. I had plenty of spending money with the business booming and drove all the way there in a Triumph Spitfire (1 PO). It was a great holiday, with the exception of hearing some shattering news on Radio Luxembourg one evening. They said on one of the news programmes, that the trading in personalised car registrations had been stopped. I couldn't believe my ears, in fact I wondered if the French wine was stronger than I'd imagined. I kept the radio on until the next news item. Then sure enough, my ears hadn't deceived me, the system of transfer of personalised plates had been stopped in Great Britain.

The next day, I phoned my office and had the news confirmed again. We certainly had problems, the Civil Service Unions had blacked all work on transfers. It was a catastrophe. I cut short my holiday and returned to England to try to sort the mess out.

The only consolation was that my Local Taxation Office at Trowbridge, were not sympathetic to the Union action. Most of the staff were members of NALGO, who refused to join the strike. A few transfers filtered through, which didn't meet with the approval of some of the LTO staff. My business was at a virtual standstill. I had to continue paying my staff and pay rent. They were dark days, although, as you may remember, the summer of 1976 was glorious. I spent most of my time playing tennis. I continually believed that the strike would end any day, however, as the temperature stayed in the seventies, work seemed to be less important.

The dealers called a meeting at a hotel in the Midlands. Everyone was there, all driving expensive cars with distinctive number plates (at least ten Rolls-Royces), it was quite a treat for the locals. The consensus of opinion was that it would all be settled shortly, but just in case, a campaign office should be started. Dealers would man the office on a rota basis.

By September, things were becoming rather serious. I was running out of cash, as a result of having to refund clients and my stock lay dormant. Andrew Stevens became impatient and decided to leave the firm. As October approached, the dealers' stand became stronger and a protest march was organised in London. Norman Fowler M.P., Shadow Transport Minister, gave his full support and addressed the marchers in Battersea Park. The demonstration was covered by both national television channels. Still the pressure wasn't enough to move the stubborn Unions. Three weeks after the London demo', I started my own campaign. I didn't believe that the dealers were being hard enough on the powers that be. My campaign started when I decided to give my Local Taxation Office one of my numbers. If they wouldn't let me transfer the registration, they may as well have it. So I got into my old clothes and dragged an oily old moped up

the steps of the Trowbridge County Hall, a commissionaire held the door open for me, and I dragged it into the taxation office. The staff were astounded, they all knew me as a sensible sort of person and there I was with this rusty old moped and a length of chain, securing the vehicle to their counter. The escapade had attracted two television crews and several reporters. You can probably imagine the scene. They vacated their desks and held an emergency meeting. One irate female civil servant, whom I happened to live near, flipped her lid. "Get that thing out of here", she kept screaming. After fifteen minutes, I decided that the mission had been achieved and I dragged the moped back to a waiting van and took it back to the farm.

Chaining the moped to the L.T.O. counter.

Although my local M.P., also tried to help resolve the strike, an end was still not in sight. In mid November, I reached the height of desperation. I informed DVLC and the media that unless the strike was called off, I would chain myself up, outside the Licensing Centre at Swansea. The strike continued, so one cold morning I drove up to Swansea armed with megaphone, placards, chain and padlock. The media were already there in force, as were security guards. They kept telling me that I couldn't use the megaphone. I ignored them and chained myself to a lamp post outside the main gate to DVLC. A few other dealers and some friends joined in the demo'. The presence of television, radio and the press, resulted in the big chiefs issuing an on the spot statement. The dispute had been settled.

No sooner were the celebrations over and the hangovers clearing, details of the Union settlement emerged. They had drawn up a set of harsh transfer rules, that in effect, made dealing in registrations almost an impossibility. A registration could not be transferred until it had been owned for nine months or more. The facility to "retain" a number had been abolished. The fee was to be increased by over 900%. However, the worst of all, transfers were not permitted from mopeds and motorcycles, to cars. As most dealers transferred numbers from cars to retention certificates or to mopeds and motorcycles for storage purposes (it was far easier than keeping hundreds of cars), the strike may as well have continued. The only concession was a six week period of grace, to transfer all registrations held on retention certificates. Although it did release some stock, the prices had to be "give away". It was either that, or transfer them to a stock of taxed and MOT'd cars. I did manage to sell every single number on retention, although it was just a case of recovering money outlayed five or more months earlier. To give you an idea of the silly asking prices, the advertisement (below), appeared in The Sunday Times on 5th December 1976. Most numbers were on retention. (The telephone number in the advertisement is no longer in use.)

Like many other dealers, I had advertised, in the good old days, for registration numbers. The majority came from cars and to save buying the cars, I would just post the documents of a moped to the vendor, to enable the number to be transferred to it. Consequently, I had a stock of mopeds that had registrations worth over £20,000, attached to them. Not one of them

could be transferred. The harsh rules made trading almost impossible. My only hope of survival was to get transfers back from mopeds and motorcycles to cars. I started another campaign and had immediate sympathy from the press.

1 ARU on one of my mopeds.

After weeks of writing to M.P.s and to DVLC, I wasn't getting any nearer to a solution. It was time for another chaining up demo'. This time I organised it to be outside the House of Commons. It was a cold day in March, when I travelled up to London by train, with a friend. We put two placards in the guard's van and discussed strategy during the journey. When we reached Paddington Station, we must have looked a right pair of "Charlies", carrying the placards through the crowds, on to the Tube. The rush hour was still on and we weren't exactly the most popular of commuters. We walked the short distance from the Underground Station to the Houses of Parliament, however, as we turned into Parliament Square, we could see a mass of reporters and Police at the very spot we had planned the demo'. The only possible alternative was opposite the St. Stephen's entrance. My friend wrapped the chain around me and through the railings, securing it with a padlock. Within seconds a throng of people dashed across the road, News At Ten, the lot. Burly Policemen barged through the mass of reporters and TV crews. One of them carried a gigantic pair of wire cutters, (that later turned out to be the same ones used to cut Emily Pankhurst's chains). It was all too much for my friend, he ran off, with the key to the padlock and the return train tickets. The Police gave me a few minutes to end the demo' or to be arrested. As I was taken away to a waiting Police car, the cameras had a field day. At Canon Row Police Station, I was charged with obstruction and bailed to appear at Bow Street Magistrates Court the following day. The Police didn't seem to take me too seriously and treated me well. They found my friend for me and we headed back to Wiltshire, minus chains and placards (they had been retained as evidence). They did let me keep the number plate I had hanging round my neck (UP U 2).

The next day at Bow Street Court, another mass of reporters were there to cover the story. In the event, I pleaded guilty to obstruction and was fined £10. Later that day, the transfer rules were changed. The waiting period had been reduced from nine months to three months and most important of all, it was now possible to transfer registration marks from mopeds and motorcycles to cars. My stock had been released, I was back in business. The eight months of fighting the bureaucrats, had paid off.

No sooner was I over that hurdle, then Frank Boniface became fed up with all the mopeds and cars being on his farm, I can't say I blame him, on reflection. People kept knocking at his door asking to buy spare parts. It was almost a scrap yard. We didn't fall out over it. I accepted the situation and found some premises on a trading estate in Westbury. The rent was crippling, it was 15,000 square feet of covered storage, workshop and car parking area. It took about a week to move the mopeds.

Although I had won a round against the bureaucrats, over the mopeds to cars ruling, they still kept an ace up their sleeves, by insisting that all the mopeds had to be taxed and MOT'd before the numbers could be transferred to cars. Of course, many of the vehicles were in very poor condition, (it hadn't mattered in the past). I was therefore forced to take on two full time mechanics to restore the vehicles as and when I sold the numbers. It was an expensive operation but I was determined not to be defeated and the business started ticking over.

For the next two years, business was slow, one of the major problems being the almost un-workable set of rules that not only the public had to suffer, but the Civil Servants also had to operate. Numerous transfers were lost for one reason or another. I had the distinct impression that the majority of Local Vehicle Licensing Offices were totally against people such as myself, trying to earn honest money from the transfer of car numbers. Their stupid rules created so much work for them that it was hardly

surprising they became frustrated. They couldn't very well make life easier for themselves without helping dealers. They were in a catch 22 situation.

In 1978 I was lucky enough to be offered the registration MAD 1. I had been pestering the owner for some time and although he had owned it for twenty five years, he had become fed up with the Civil Servants nonsense over transfers and decided to sell it. The number was perfect for me. I paid £750 for it, willingly and believed I had the bargain of the year. I bought a brand new Datsun 260Z sports car, to put the number on. It was a real eye catcher and a very comfortable car. The number attracted a lot of publicity and served as an advertising medium. I kept MAD 1 on the Datsun until the day I had a head on collision with another car (registration number "WAM"). Nobody was hurt in the accident, but as the Datsun was severely damaged I had to find another car quickly for MAD 1. I bought a Rolls Royce Silver Shadow and had the number transferred to it within a matter of days.

About this time, I got involved with a local pop group. I was acting as agent for them and commissioned them to make a record for me, all about my car number escapades. The group was "Graduate" from Bath. The song was quite catchy and included such lyrics as "chained to a sidewalk, shaking his fist at the people walking by, don't try to stop him with your lofty legislation". It was written by Roland Orzabal and I bought the copyright from him. Although the record didn't get anywhere in the charts, "Graduate" did offer me the chance to be their manager if I put up something like £4000. I wasn't prepared to risk such an amount, although their original manager did. It could have been one of the biggest mistakes of my life. The group split up but Roland Orzabal and Curt Smith kept going and renamed themselves "Tears for Fears". Their first Album went to number one in the charts and turned over in excess of one million pounds. Whether or not I could have had a slice of the action, no-one knows. I doubt it, because the chap who managed them, was rumoured to have ended up taking a second mortgage on his house and losing a small fortune. In any case the contract expired just before Roland and Curt hit the big time. I can at least have the satisfaction of being involved in a top group from the early adventurous days. At least I still have Roland's first recorded work, signed and sealed.

As 1980 approached and we had a change of Government, I was encouraged to invest more time and energy into the business. It soon began to pay off and business started to improve. Transfers seemed to be going through more easily and DVLC accepted the situation that the "three months rule" was being avoided by the "donor" becoming the keeper of the "recipient" vehicle, (on paper). All was well, until some high and mighty Civil Servants, employed at the London Enforcement Office, (a branch of the Dept. of Transport), decided that DVLC should not be accepting such transfers. It was obvious that departments were clashing. The L.E.O., were determind to use their powers to override DVLC and to stop dealers and the public from avoiding the three months ruling. As a result of numerous telephone conversations with them, I was under no illusion, the conceited bunch, were a serious threat to business. The more I stirred them up, the more attentive they became. They started to pull my transfer applications out of different Licensing Offices and set about voiding the numbers, because of irregularities in the applications. Their procedure was to send two officers to my client's house, (the donor), and to introduce themselves, waving a warrant card in front of my client's face. "We are officers of the London Enforcement Office . . . we must warn you that anything you say may be taken down and used in evidence against you". I know how I would feel if this suddenly happened to me, I'd be shocked. After all, these people were only selling a car number plate and were supposedly dealing with an experienced firm. The result was that most of them panicked, believing that they had committed an offence, by signing the transfer papers. Some of them said that they hadn't signed the paper. It was all the more ammunition for the cold blooded bureaucrats. The prime time for calling on my customers was around 7 pm. The cases were far from isolated and I lost many transfers and sales. One client was in tears when she phoned me. Her family were worried to death, she wanted to get out of the deal straight away. I had no choice but to write it, and many others off, just to save the anxiety of my clients. I complained bitterly. I was obviously being victimised and it was time to fight them. Using one case as a precedent, I challenged the Dept. of Transport to justify their actions or face me in Court. To my surprise, I was offered the opportunity of a meeting at DVLC, Swansea. I asked them if it would be possible to bring David Kempson along to the meeting with me, (CNDA Secretary), they agreed and the date was set for 15th April.

David and I had an air of confidence as we walked into the plush meeting room, many floors up the white (elephant) edifice. Richard Bayly, (head of DVLC Policy Vehicles Section), introduced Mr. Blakemore and Mr. Molyneaux from his Department and the head of the London Enforcement Office, Mr, C.H.T. Davies. There I was, face to face with the man who was hell bent on making my customers life a misery. I managed to control myself and not soak him with one of the flasks of water provided by the bureaucrats. I even managed to conduct my conversation in a civilised manner. It was quite an achievement, considering the damage that had been done. The minutes of the meeting are as follows:-

PURPOSE OF MEETING
1. Mr Bayly explained that he had suggested the meeting because of Mr Hill's concern about his relationship with the Department and its handling of cherished transfer cases in which he had an interest. It would not be possible at the meeting to discuss the Minister's review of cherished transfers.

2. Mr Hill drew attention to a letter from a LVLO to one of his clients which sets out information on how transfers were possible. Mr Hill considered the letter to be accurate . Officials, after reading the letter, explained that while it was, strictly, accurate some of the terms used were open to ambiguity. It was therefore agreed that it would be helpful to discuss the points which it raised.

KEEPERSHIP
3. Mr Hill said that the letter implied that both cars involved in transfers had to be "owned" by the same person. Mr Bayly explained that while this was strictly true the legal definition "owner" in the relevant law was "the keeper of the vehicle". The use of the word "owner" in the context of cherished transfers was not, therefore, intended to imply the legal owner of a vehicle. It was agreed that this situation could be confusing to the public but, given the way the law was drafted, there was no way round it.

4. It was agreed that the term "keeper" was difficult to define. Ultimately it was for the

Courts to interpret legal meanings of this kind but in the absence of any judgement of a Court both the Department and members of the public involved in transfers had to make a reasonable assessment of what the law intended. For its part the Department considered there were some cases of transfers where the concept was being abused. For example forged signatures on Registration Documents suggested genuine abuse of the system. However this did not mean that all examples of so called "reversed transfers" constituted abuse. It was for all the parties involved in transfers to assure themselves that the declarations which they made were true. The Department could not give clear guidance to cover every case.

DELAYS
5. Mr Hill expressed concern at the delays which took place on transfers at LVLOs, particularly over inspections. Mr Kempson mentioned the particular difficulty of getting vehicles inspected when they were taken to the LVLOs on trailers.

6. Mr Bayly explained that it should be understood that a LVLO's priorities were first licensing and registration and secondly enforcement. Work on cherished transfers had to give precedence to these. Mr. Davies explained the delays at some offices, particularly at some times of the month were inevitable. He stressed that the onus was on the applicant to produce a vehicle for inspection at a place and in a manner requested by the Department. However, if problems were encountered he suggested that the Office Manager or Area Manager should be consulted. In the final resort he would be prepared to look into special problems himself.

PENALTIES
7. Mr Blakemore said that the legal penalty or a fine of up to £1,000 or 2 years imprisonment was contained in Section 26 of the Vehicle Excise Act 1971 and covered false declarations. However officials explained that penalties of this kind would be unliklely to be used against such members of the public who had unwittingly made minor errors while completing forms. It was available to counter deliberate and serious cases of abuse.

GENERAL
8. Mr Hill was concerned that cases of transfers with which he was associated were being singled out for special treatment by LVLOs. Mr Davies assured him that all applications for transfers were, as far as possible, given equal treatment. There was, inevitably, some variation of approach to transfers generally from office to office, which the Department did its best to remove, but there should not be any difference of treatment between individual members of the public. Mr Davies agreed to look into any particular cases where Mr Hill considered he had been wrongly treated if the details were given to him.

9. Mr Bayly stressed that while the Department recognised the service dealers could provide to the public as advisors in transfer cases, applications had to be made by the keepers of the vehicle concerned.
Any queries over the applications had to be taken to the applicants themselves. The Department could not act through dealers as intermediaries. Mr Hill and Mr Kempson accepted this.

10. In conclusion Mr Bayly said that the regulations covering cherished transfers did make it difficult to give precise advice on what was and what was not permissible. Each case had to be treated separately on its merits. However the notes on the back of the application aimed to give clear guidance. He would welcome advice at any time on how and/or why they might be confusing. Officials would also be willing at any time to look into any other specific worries or concerns which Mr Hill or Mr Kempson might have.

11. Mr Hill and Mr Kempson thanked officials for the opportunity to discuss the problems raised and stressed their interest in consultation on any proposals which the Minister might bring forward as a result of the current review.

(Reproduced by kind permission of D.V.L.C.).

I was very pleased with the outcome of the meeting. Richard Bayly had put the Department's case fairly and squarely, at the same time acknowledging the existence and respectability of most of the leading dealers. It was a major step forward in relations with DVLC. However, the L.E.O., weren't giving up, One of the cases they were pursuing was that of a Mrs Hodgkinson who had been visited by the burly Enforcement Officers and had made a statement to them disclaiming a signature on my client's registration document. I was 100% sure that nobody in my office would forge her signature and it would be most unlikely that a friend or relation or an escaped document forger, would have signed it. I knew it could only be her signature and that she had been frightened into saying it wasn't. The L.E.O., told her that she would lose the number altogether, as a result of her statement. I wrote to the L.E.O., on 21st April, asking them to explain the impending accusation. I was convinced that because of the hundreds of wasted man hours, that had resulted from the preoccupation of bizarre bureaucrats, they had to justify their existence and carry out a prosecution. It was really quite a worrying time, as I knew that at the end of the day, a judge and jury were far more likely to listen to the plausible arguments of people in respected positions, than to take the side of little me, who makes a living out of changing over car number plates.

The L.E.O., letter in reply to mine, is reproduced below and I am sure you will realise just how intent the "little Hitlers" were;

Department of Transport

Driver and Vehicle Licensing

London Enforcement Office 3 Hanover Street London W1R 9HH

Telephone 01 - 734 6010 ext

Mr A J Hill Elite Registrations PO Box 1 Bradford-on-Avon Wiltshire BA15 1YQ	Your reference AJH/AS/6392MP Our reference LO/CHTD Date 30 April 1980

Dear Mr Hill

1.   I am replying to your letter of 21 April (with enclosure) and concerning the Department's refusal to permit the transfer of registration mark 6392 MP from a Ford Popular saloon to a Triumph Stag saloon. The application for this transfer was made by a Mrs J G Hodgkinson; from the comments you made to me at Swansea on 15 April and the fact that you have produced a photo copy of Mr M Davies letter of 31 March 1980 to Mrs Hodgkinson I assume that she is the client you refer to. You will appreciate I am sure that the transfer transaction was between the Department and Mrs Hodgkinson; the information I now supply is to make it clear to you that the Department has firm ground for refusal of this transfer.

2.   The refusal is not because of a falsified signature on form V317 and Mr M Davies letter of 31 March does not make this claim. The application was refused, following enquiries into discrepancies in the documents, because Mrs Hodgkinson has formally stated that she has at no time been the keeper of the recipient vehicle (the Triumph Stag); and that, furthermore, she did not sign the declaration on form V5 for this vehicle which purported to transfer the vehicle to her keepership. Rule (c) on the reverse of form V317 sets out the condition.

3.   It is now necessary to pursue enquiries as to whether an offence in respect of Section 26 of the Vehicles (Excise) Act 1971 may have been committed, and retention of the documentation is required to enable these enquiries to be made. So that she may have use of or be able to dispose of the Ford Popular Mrs Hodgkinson has been offered the opportunity to obtain a fresh registration mark to replace 6392 MP. I trust this explanation clarifies the situation to you.

Yours sincerely

C H T DAVIES   10

A further letter form the L.E.O., stated "I regret to inform you that due to irregularities which occured at the time the transaction was submitted to our Local Office and in view of the statement made to our Inquiry Officers, I have no alternative but to reject your application for transfer and make void the registration mark 6392 MP".

I challenged their decision by referring to the terms and conditions of transfer as detailed on the form V317 issued by the Dept. of Transport. Section 5 states; "if for any reason a transfer is authorised in circumstances which do not accord with the conditions of transfer, the transferred mark may subsequently be made void". I argued that as the transfer application had NOT YET been authorised, the L.E.O., were not in a position to void the mark. I won the round and they not only relented on the voiding issue, but permitted the transfer. Naturally I did supsect that they would turn around and say that as the application for transfer had now BEEN authorised, they could now void the number. However, their petty minded bureaucracy had obviously "gone over the top", and nobody has heard a word from them since.

In October 1980, Manchester Council offered a distinctive number one, registration for sale. They invited tenders and naturally I was interested. I wrote to the LVLO in the Council area and asked if they could explain to me how it was possible to transfer such a registration. The letter I received contained exactly the opposite information that the L.E.O. had spent so much time fighting about. It was clear acceptance that DVLC approved of the system of the donor temporarily being the keeper of the recipient vehicle, purely for the purpose of the transfer, and therefore avoiding the three months ruling. At long last I was able to carry out my business with reduced pressure and more efficiently and effectively.

As business began to look up again, I decided to invest in a lease of a yard near Bradford-on-Avon, . It had previously been a scrap yard, but hadn't traded as such for a year or so. There was plenty of space to store cars, motorcycles and mopeds, it was perfect for the numbers business, and within only a few months it was half full of vehicles. The problem was that word soon spread that the old scrap yard was in action again, and without any advertising, I was in the second hand car spares and scrap metal business. It was going

so well, that I registered a business name (Melksham Breakers) and employed a full time chap (Percy Henley), to run the business. He was experienced in the second hand car spares trade and was great at the work. He was just the sort of person you would expect to find at a car scrap

yard. He turned an old shed into his office and canteen, not exactly The Ritz, (although it was to him) and he enjoyed every second of it. The business boomed, which unfortunately, was to prove his downfall. It was so successful that it became a thriving scrap business and took up all the space in the yard. I had no choice but to scrap the scrap to make room for vehicles with numbers. Percy moved into another scrap yard and I employed the services of a chap called Ed. Together, we flattened all the cars in the yard, with the assistance of a Priestman Crane, which had actually been condemned unfit for use by a Crane Inspector. We had gigantic bonfires that lit up the sky for miles around. After several weeks, the yard was clear again and I was out of the scrap business. Although I learnt a lot about metals, I was pleased to see the back of the business.

Meanwhile, in late 1980, I decided to have a go at starting a car numbers newspaper. I called it Car Numbers Monthly. To build up customers, I gave thousands of copies away, free of charge. Despite considerable losses in the early days, the paper exists to this day and usually manages to break even.

About the time of the launch of Car Numbers Monthly, I had the most shattering experience of my career. Two officers from Customs & Excise, VAT Investigation Division, called at my office. I was under suspicion of tax evasion. The two "Gestapo" type officers fired question after question at me, trying to make me admit to the offence. It would be an understatement to say that I was shocked. As they turned my office upside down, searching every drawer and every filing cabinet, it was obvious that they meant business. Although they had warned me that anything I said, may be taken down and used in evidence, it didn't stop me telling them anything they wanted to know. I had never deliberately attempted to evade VAT. They told me that two other officers were simultaneously "raiding" my yard. I phoned "Percy" who confirmed this and who was obviously in his element, being totally unco-operative with them. They had grilled him, demanding to know where all the papers were hidden. As no incriminating evidence existed anywhere, I told Percy to help them and he thoroughly enjoyed taking them on a guided tour of the muddy and oily yard helping them open the boots of over one hundred cars. Eventually they settled for thousands of documents from my office and took them away in two cars.

The raid shouldn't have come as a surprise, as I had heard of similar cases with other dealers and fines of £10,000 being imposed, forcing them out of business. They had been going through numerous dealers, with the assistance of DVLC Swansea, who provided reams of copy documents of vehicles registered to the dealer. I was now in the same boat and I knew that my VAT records were far from satisfactory. However, as no VAT officer had ever complained about the appalling book keeping, I had never bothered to change the system.

Several weeks later, they called me into their office in Bristol to help sort the mess out. I couldn't believe it, they had allocated a whole room to my case. Rows of filing cabinets contained the documents they had taken from me and items such as old cheque books were in polythene bags in a corner of the room. They told me that they had been through my advertisements and found the numbers that I had been selling. They had obtained copies of the registration documents for each one from DVLC. However, they were still unable to pinpoint an exact figure to extract from me. They even quizzed me on how much I had made from the sale of RR 1. This was possibly the turning point, as I realised that they were resorting to guess work. I had never been involved with the sale of RR 1, the owner had purchased it in 1968! However, I was doing a story on it, for Car Numbers Monthly and the

paper work on the item, was part of their haul. I demanded the return of my papers, after all they had not come up with any proof of tax evasion. They agreed to let me have photo-copies of all the documents. I estimated over 20,000 individual pieces of paper. It took them a week to do the photo-copies and they delivered them to me in a van.

Their task was to ensure that I had made VAT payments on every car number that I had sold. They were also not happy that I had de-registered my VAT liability during the hard times of 1978/ 1979. They had a mammoth task and after almost a year of arguing, they still couldn't work out any substantial discrepancy. They then turned their attention to my original date of registration for VAT and started looking for payments as far back as the days with Pop. After fourteen months, they presented me with a bill for £8,000, however they failed to produce concrete evidence of the transactions involved in such a sum. The only discrepancy in my accounts, turned out to be a period when my customers were not charged VAT, when they should have been. I estimated this amount to £2,500 and made them an offer they couldn't refuse. If they permitted me to ask the customers involved, to pay me the VAT, I would pay them this amount of £2,500. They told me that they don't haggle, they wanted £8,000, full stop. For the next few weeks they tried hard with increased pressure on me. I told them where to go and within a few days they accepted my offer and signed a document stating that all VAT was accounted for, to date, and permitted me to ask my customers for the unpaid VAT. I am convinced that they were very disappointed not to have found me to be the naughty boy that they had suspected in the first place. Their enquiries must have cost well in excess of £5000, perhaps they'll think twice before suspecting me again.

The latter end of 1980 proved to be action packed for me. Transfers were going through, although a most unpleasant atmosphere existed with many of the Local Vehicle Licensing Offices. The transfer rules that had been drawn up in 1976, with an obvious view to crack the business of dealing in numbers, had slowly back-fired on the petty minded bureaucrats. I was convinced that they were upset by the apparent ease of overcoming the harsh transfer rules. Consequently, when my clients approached many LVLO's to carry out a transfer, numerous obstacles would be put in the way, to try to put the client off the deal. I lost many sales because of such action and naturally, I complained to DVLC, Swansea. However, they kept asking for concrete evidence of such animosity and unfortunately, I wasn't able to supply such, without written proof. The clever civil servants made sure that attacks on dealers were kept to a verbal nature, until one day, when one of them finally went too far.

A client phoned me to say that he had received a phone call from the manager of the Shrewsbury LVLO, implying that he shouldn't deal with my firm. Fortunately, my client had the forethought to ask the manager to put his reasoning in writing and incredibly, for the first time, I obtained written proof of the existence of the malice that I had been complaining about.

The letter to my client reads as follows:-

"May I please refer you to my telephone conversation of some weeks ago, when I explained that the applications received from Elite Registrations have to be scrutinised most thoroughly as it has been found that in practically **all** cases reveived from this firm, the "cherished transfer" has not even taken place. This firm apparently advertises for registration numbers in the national press, which is quite **illegal** and it has been found that the donor vehicle either does not exist, having been previously scrapped, or remains in the original keeper's possession – the **number only** being transferred. It is of great concern to most Managers of Local Vehicle Licensing Offices that this state of affairs exists and I am sure I am correct in stating that all Managers would welcome some form of legislation which would debar such illegal transactions taking place".

I took the letter straight to my Solicitor, who advised me to obtain Counsel opinion. After a few weeks wait, Counsel advised; "Elite Registrations are accused in this letter of running an illegal business or, at the very least, running a legal business in an illegal manner, This is quite clearly defamatory. Bearing in mind that the Plaintiff trades on his own account as Elite Registrations, there is no difficulty in proving that the words used referred to him and his firm".

Whilst I had been waiting for the legal advice, I kept quiet about the letter but once I was satisfied that a foolproof case existed, I informed DVLC of my intention to sue the Department for damages in respect of defamation. At long last I was able to say "there you are, now do you believe me?" The reaction was profound apology from them. However, that was not good enough for me, I wanted my pound of flesh.

In fairness to DVLC, they took the matter extremely seriously and agreed to meet me in London, to discuss it.

I trotted up to London and entered the towering offices of the Department of Transport in Marsham Street. I was given the VIP treatment at reception and taken to a conference room, many floors up. I wasn't nervous, as I knew the strength of my case, in fact I was extremely interested to gauge their reaction. The conference room was empty, although meticulously laid out for five places. Within a few minutes the door opened and a rather solemn gentleman entered, impeccably dressed. He announced himself as the D.O.T., legal adviser who was responsible for draughting the cherished transfer rules in late 1976. I was momentarily stunned, "was this the idiot who had devised or approved the set of rules that had almost put me out of business, and caused considerable inconvenience and distress to thousands of motorists?" In the heat of the moment I replied, "how long did you spend on that, ten minutes?" I was enraged, that the D.O.T., had the gall to send this person above all others to settle me in to the meeting. It was a deliberate ploy to un-nerve me prior to the commencement of the meeting. It didn't work and it had the opposite effect. It settled me into the meeting with an air of determination. Shortly afterwards, the other officials entered the room. Richard Bayly (head of DVLC, Policy), chaired the meeting. I explained my position and concluded by asking for a cool £20,000 damages. They replied that damages would be paid to me, but not to that amount. I would receive an offer in writing within a few weeks. They also discussed the operation of the cherished transfer system in general and I was able to put comments and suggestions forward. I left the meeting, well satisfied.

For the next few months we haggled over an amount for damages. I reflected on the situation and decided not to take the matter to court. It would have wasted too much time and as I was sure to win the case, I felt that the delicate situation at many LVLO's over their attitude to cherished transfers, could possibly become more strained, if one of their own, was dragged through the courts. I settled for £250 damages and a letter of apology to myself and my client. That letter concluded; "I have examined the papers in detail and I would like to point out that there is no justification for these allegations, being applied to the firm Elite Registrations".

It has been particularly noticeable that since the defamation affair, LVLO staff have been most careful not to incriminate themselves. They seem to have accepted that cherished numbers are here to stay and although pockets of dissent exist to this day, the general attitude has become more favourable.

In March 1981 the Secretary of State for Transport issued a consultation paper detailing sweeping changes to the cherished transfer rules. It had been a long wait for "the promised land" and it was better late than never. Since the Conservatives came to power in 1979, I had continually demanded that they change the unworkable set of rules, that the Labour Government had approved. I used Car Numbers Monthly as the front line of attack and readers contributed with their own criticisms. The CNDA and RNC also fought hard for a change of rules. At long last, we could all now see the official view of the transfer scene. The full text of the consultation paper is reproduced as follows:-

1. More and more motorists are becoming interested in keeping or obtaining particular registration numbers. These are sometimes called "cherished numbers". The purpose of this consultation paper is to obtain the views of the public and interested bodies on ways to make it easier for motorists to do this.

2. At the moment anyone acquiring an attractive number for the first time, or transferring one to another car, has to comply with a set of rules. These were originally drawn up to prevent the record from being confused; in practice, they have proved extremely tortuous and have involved the public in considerable difficulty.

3. The Secretary of State for Transport sees no reason why, motorists who prefer to keep particular numbers for their vehicles should not do so as long as the registration records remain clear and a fee is paid for the service. He believes that the present rules are unnecessarily complicated and inconvenient and he would like to offer a simpler service.

Ending the Validity of Old "Log Books"

4. As a first step towards simplifying the rules all the registration numbers still in use should be properly entered on the computer record at the Driver and Vehicle Licensing Centre (DVLC) Swansea. The vast majority are already on the record. It has the details of all those vehicles, over 26 million, which have been issued with new style, blue and white registration documents (with the number V5 in the top right hand corner). However, there are still some vehicles which have not yet been taken on to DVLC's records. Mostly these will be old vehicles which have been off the road for three years or more but have not been destroyed. The details of these vehicles can usually only be confirmed by the old style green cardboard registration documents, often called "log books".

5. In order to establish their entitlement to a particular number, many owners of such vehicles have voluntarily put the registration details on the DVLC record. But some have not and up to now it has been possible to revive an old number by producing a vehicle to which it may once have belonged. If the record were complete it would be possible for the Secretary of State to consider re-issuing old registration marks which people would like to acquire. This is not possible now since the mark may still exist on a car in someone's garage .

6. The Secretary of State proposes, therefore, to end the process of transferring vehicle registration records to the DVLC computer under old registration numbers. Anyone who wanted to keep the old number of a vehicle which was not recorded at Swansea would need to take, or send the old green "log book" to a Local Vehicle Licensing Office before a set date. This would need to be done for any vehicle, even if it was in a museum, laid up or being restored. Vehicles do **not** have to be in a road-worthy condition before the records be registered at DVLC. People wanting to keep their old "log books" for historical or sentimental reasons would have them returned by DVLC on request.

7. Subject to the outcome of this consultation a final date would be set allowing a period of 3 months to give people who have not already done so, a last chance to retain their old registration numbers by registering their vehicles at DVLC. As at present, evidence that the vehicle still existed and that the number claimed was appropriate would be needed.

8. After the end of the 3 month period anyone wanting to use on the road a vehicle which was not recorded at DVLC would have to re-register it under a replacement number. Unless there were exceptional reasons, vehicles would then lose entitlement to their original number.

Possible changes to the Transfer Rules

9. Once it becomes possible to check from the computer record what registration numbers are already in use it will be possible to sweep away many of the existing bureaucratic rules and replace them with a simple guide.

Transfers between different owners

10. For the public the most difficult of all the current requirements is that when a number is transferred both of the vehicles involved must be registered in the name of the same "keeper" (or owner). In most cases this means that anyone buying a new car and wishing to keep the registration number from his old one has to own both cars – until the transfer of the number can be arranged. If this rule were removed, straightforward transfers could be allowed between different vehicles, irrespective of who owned them. This would help people acquiring interesting numbers for the first time and those changing their car but wanting to keep the same number. The Secretary of State proposes to abolish this rule.

Transfers between different kinds of vehicles.

11. At present transfers are not allowed from cars on to motor cycles, or between certain other vehicles taxation classes. There seems to be little purpose in this rule. The Secretary of State therefore proposes to end it.

Stolen vehicles

12. Under the present rules people whose cars are stolen lose entitlement to their numbers. Confusion would be caused if the number of a stolen car reappeared on a new one soon after the theft, but it seems harsh to insist that marks from stolen cars should be lost for ever. The Secretary of State therefore would like to re-issue these marks if the vehicles are not recovered after a period of time. The waiting period should be long enough to prevent confusion with records of stolen vehicles, but no longer.

The three-month rule

13. A vehicle has to be registered in one person's name for more than 3 months before he can have its number transferred to another vehicle. This rule is probably unnecessary in the way it is operated at present, but it is important to ensure that once a mark has been transferred, it is not transferred again until Departmental and police records have been brought up to date. The Secretary of State believes that the best way to achieve this would be to impose a temporary limit on re-transferring a mark for a short time – and 3 months still seems the best interval – after it is transferred. This should not cause difficulties to the ordinary motorists and should prevent vehicle records from becoming confused.

Licensing "period of grace"

14. The present rule that both vehicles involved in a transfer have to be licensed can cause difficulties when one of the vehicles is damaged in an accident or fails the MOT test. Entitlement to a particular mark should not be affected by uncertainties of this kind. The Secretary of State therefore proposes to allow a period of grace after the expiry of a licence during which a transfer can still take place.

Vehicle inspection

15. At present all vehicles from which numbers are being transferred have to be physically inspected by Departmental officials or the police. Inspections are made to ensure that the vehicles involved really exist, that they are not stolen vehicles masquerading under a different number, and that the transfer is not taking place against the will of their owners. To end inspections completely would open the door to considerable fraud. But they are very often inconvenient for the public as well as diverting police or civil service manpower. Because of this the Secretary of State proposes to relax the requirements for inspection in cases where there is little possiblity of abuse – for example when a vehicle from which a number is being taken has been **licensed and registered** by the same person for more than a year. This would reduce the need for inspections by 70% to 80% and would give an improved service to most ordinary motorists with cherished numbers.

"Off-the-peg" marks

16. The law does not allow numbers to be retained separately from vehicles. This means

15

that motorists may encounter difficulties through having to keep their old car until they have a new one on to which they can transfer their cherished number. A new scheme which allowed marks to be retained, for a short period, off a car in return for a special charge would require legislation. Because of this it cannot be introduced at once but an 'off-the-peg' scheme appears to be a desirable feature of an improved transfer service. The Secretary of State is prepared to consider a change of this kind when legislative time is available if there is a demand for it.

17. Changing the rules in these ways would make it easier for people with cherished numbers to retain them, and would help those wanting to obtain one for the first time to acquire, by agreement, a number already used on someone else's vehicle. In addition to this there will be many attractive old numbers no longer in existence. The Secretary of State has no firm plans to reallocate these marks. But he is open to suggestions on whether re-issuing old marks, or even selling them would be a good idea.

Consultation
18. Before coming to decisions on the proposed changes the Secretary of State wishes to study the view of the public and all interested bodies on the present transfer system and how it might be improved.

Norman Folwers's proposals were generally welcomed with a few reservations. I was relieved that an end was in sight, to the tortuous set of rules that had been suffered for the past five years.

No sooner had the good news of possible changes, been delivered, the civil servants decided to have another strike. Although the LVLO staff didn't join in, cherished transfers suffered, as they were not being processed at DVLC and documentation required for cherished transfer (donor and recipient V 5 documents) were not materialising. The dispute disrupted my business for more than three months.

In February 1981, I received my first fine for a motoring offence. I was caught speeding in my Rolls-Royce doing 43 mph in a 30 mph limit in Salisbury. I was actually on my way to my cousin's wedding when I committed the evil deed.

My brother, who was luckily armed with his camera, took the photograph below, of the actual moment of being "pinched by the law". My mother was also in the car at the time, but not wanting to be in the picture, she ran off down the road, clutching a gigantic floppy hat (her pride and joy for the wedding day). It must have been quite a sight. There was the shining Rolls, with MAD 1 on the number plate, the poor old Bobby, trying to do his job whilst my brother was taking roll after roll of photographs to capture the event and of course my mother in her best prim and tucker, running away. Within minutes of me being nabbed, my brother had sold one of the photographs to The Sun newspaper, over the telephone, for £100. Naturally, on the day of the case, I had to make the most of it, after all it was being covered by several national newspapers, TV and radio. The magistrate was not amused when I asked for time to pay the £25 fine. However, the story had entertained millions of people, so I wasn't exactly distressed.

As 1981 progressed, I began to trade in agricultural vehicles with interesting registration numbers. A friend of mine, Alan Pettitt, owned a farm and it made sense to join forces with him to trade in such vehicles. We formed a business partnership and started filling one of his fields with tractors and other vehicles. Although these vehicles were not subject to MOT, there was still a difficulty in transfer, because each one had to be taken to an LVLO for inspeciton of the chassis number. This involved a round trip of sixty miles and in my opinion, a total waste of time, because the inspecting officer was usually a member of the LVLO staff, who couldn't identify a tractor chassis number from a telephone number. One

Licensing Office even insisted that a Combine Harvester be taken to the office for the inspection farce. I complained bitterly, that it would require a police escort for the wide load. The LVLO manager wouldn't change his mind, however, the police contacted him and eventually he changed his mind and sent one of his staff to see the vehicle. After that escapade I kept clear of Combines'. Another hazard of trading in agricultural vehicles is that most owners are farmers and notoriously difficult people to do business with. I believe that Alan should be awarded a medal for his patience in dealing with them. Between us we spent a lot of money and effort expanding the business. Alan gave up several other business interests to devote all of his time to the trade. Within a year we were well established as the forerunners of the tractor number trade. Our advertising in national farming journals inevitably led others into the market.

In November 1982 we received a bombshell. The D.O.T., announced that all tractor transfers were to be banned. We had approximately thirty working days to dispose of our stock. It was a nightmare, the worst thing that could possibly happen. It was time to enter into battle again. I met my local M.P., and he promised to do his best to help. However, the D.O.T., were adamant and not prepared to give in. They claimed that the reason for the ban was because tractors posed a health and safety risk for LVLO staff. I argued that in the majority of cases, the inspecting officer did not even have to touch the vehicle to inspect the chassis number. Most of these are clearly visible at eye level. I wrote to many M.P's and plagued DVLC with my complaints. Eventually they partially gave in and agreed to permit a six months period of grace, extending the permitted period for trading in agricultural and other vehicles exempt from MOT testing to 30th September 1983. At the time of writing this book, my intention is to vigorously fight for the resumption of a permanent facility to transfer such registrations.

Despite the issuing of the consultation paper in March 1981, by March 1982, the tortuous set of rules were still in operation and no sign of any new rules being introduced. Consequently, the numbers business didn't boom, but just ticked over acceptably. One number I was trying to sell was 1 NW for film star, Norman Wisdom. He decided to sell the number, because he now lives

on the Isle of Man and cannot use the number there. He had been keeping the number on a vehicle, that was locked up in a garage near his London flat. I had the good fortune of meeting him there. He spent two hours helping me with my stand-up comedian act. A career which I had embarked on earlier that year as an eccentric whim. I had already followed Bernard Manning's act (also featured in this book, with his number BJM 1). That was quite an experience for someone who had only been in the comedian business for four weeks. I was so hopeless, I was a reasonable success. Later that year, Esther Rantzen's show, That's Life, took me on as the World's Worst Comedian, I am just recovering from the effects of that.

On the 25th November 1982, Lynda Chalker M.P., Parliamentary Under Secretary of State for Transport, announced that "following full consultations, new streamlined arrangements would be introduced to make the transfer of vehicle registration numbers easier and simpler. The new rules to come into force on 10th January 1983, Despite the "sweeping changes" proposed by Norman Fowler in March 1981. The long wait was far from worthwhile. The only significant change was the abolition of the three months ruling and even that wasn't much of a concession. There was no return of the retention system or the facility to transfer numbers from cars to motorcycles. I discovered from DVLC the reasoning behind the latter was "the police in particular were concerned because there was evidence to suggest that in many instances stocks of motorcycle frames were being held and built up, as and when the need arose, using the same brake, engine and lighting set. This clearly goes against the spirit of the transfer scheme and also poses road safety problems. It was therefore decided not to extend the present service in respect of motorcycles particularly since it does seem to meet the needs of the majority of motorists".

This nonsense was directed squarely at people like myself, entrepreneurs and employers. I have no shame in admitting that I hold large stocks of mopeds and motorcycles in association with my car numbers business. I have been buying the vehicles for many years and two full time members of my staff, religiously spend five days a week repairing each one to MOT standard, to enable a tax disc to be obtained, which will then permit the number to be transferred, after which the tax disc is cancelled and refunded and the vehicle kept for spare parts for another of the same make. Each vehicle attains an MOT pass certificate in accordance with the requirements of the Road Traffic Act. It is passed as fit for road use, although it never actually is driven on the road. My vehicles cannot possibly be classed as road safety problems. Furthermore, if the "spirit of the transfer scheme" doesn't include making a profit, why have successive Governments approved vast increases in the transfer fee, which have resulted in considerable profit? In any case, what business is it of the police to involve themselves in the subject, without having the courtesy to consult the sectors of private industry that stand to suffer?

After a while DVLC told me which police body were responsible. It turned out to be ACPO (Association of Chief Police Officers). I wrote to them asking if they would kindly explain why they objected to a car number being transferred to a moped but not from one moped to another moped. Surely, if a road safety problem existed in transferring a number from a car to a moped, the same risk would be involved, transferring a number from a moped to another moped? I wrote to ACPO asking them for their

objections in writing. About four weeks later I received the following reply; "With regard to your letter dated 10th May. In due course it was considered by our Traffic Committee who have asked me to tell you that the ACPO objection to cherished numbers is NOT from a road safety point of view, but in relation to crime. The main problem is that the registration number does not remain with the vehicle".

The letter proved conclusively that ACPO didn't understand the cherished numbers game. However, it enabled me to prove my case to the Secretary of State for Transport. I claimed that DVLC may have been deliberately painting a false picture to the Government on this aspect of transfers. I knew that it was pure fantasy for a police body to object to transfers on road safety grounds, however, I didn't anticipate them coming forward with an alternative objection, (in relation to crime). This was even more of a fantasy and perhaps, evidence that ACPO really hadn't bothered to study the subject before involving themselves. After all, the idea of cherished transfer (which is a provision of law, approved by successive Governments), is that the registration number does NOT remain with the vehicle. There is nothing criminal in such a practise and indeed the Government make a profit from it, as well as approving it.

I am not sure when the first vehicle was stolen, but it must be a reasonable guess that by 1904 "the vehicle lifting industry" was well under way. As all vehicles used on the road, had to have registration numbers from the 1st January 1904, it would have been on, or about that date, that criminals changed the number plates of their stolen wares. They didn't apply to Local Taxation Offices, and pay the £5 transfer fee to change the registration number. No, from 1904 to date, criminals carry out illegal transfers. Whether or not a legal transfer system exists, criminals will always change the most identifiable part of the vehicle, the registration number, therefore the ACPO letter to me, must be classed as one of the most ridiculous of official replies.

Although at the time of going to press, the car to moped ban still exists, I am convinced that it is just a matter of time before the facility is reinstated.

At present the moped side of my business is restricted to buying them when they already have interesting numbers registered to them. In early 1983 DVLC instructed my LVLO to stop

18

registering these vehicles to me, unless they had supporting documents. It was not possible for me to obtain a duplicate registration document when the original had been lost by the previous owner in situations when the vehicle was not yet registered at DVLC. This change of policy was fired at me without any warning and I was unable to change their minds. I stood to loose upwards of £5000. I had the vehicles in my possession, all with the original number plates. So what objection did DVLC have this time? They claimed in their usual petty way, that someone else may have a more legitimate claim to the mark. In other words, someone could have transferred the number before 1977 but not changed the number plate on the moped. It would have been an acceptable tale of woe for them, except that they admitted to me that none of the numbers on the mopeds in dispute were registered at DVLC to any other vehicle. I asked if they could let me have different registration numbers of similar value (incidentally none of the plates had much individual value, it was just collectively that they were worth a lot of money). DVLC have millions of numbers available to them, from vehicles that have been destroyed, and from LTO series that were NEVER issued to a vehicle. Yet they miserly refused to let me have any of these numbers and to add insult to injury offered me numbers like DFD 832B, (worthless junk).

After much correspondence, I have managed to get DVLC to agree to register the numbers to me after the 30th November 1983. This is the closing date for conversion of all vehicles from the old LTO registration system to the DVLC computer.

By June 1983 as this book is going to press, the new transfer rules were beginning to settle down and believe it or not, DVLC actually going out of their way to ensure that all the LVLO's were fully conversant with the new rules. The only exception to the rule (well, there had to be one), being an arrogant member of staff at the Norwich LVLO who told me that HE made the rules and not DVLC. To cut a long story short, DVLC had approved a transfer where the donor vehicle couldn't be MOT'd again and therefore could not be taxed. The bumptious bureaucrat insisted that the donor vehicle MUST be taxed before he could complete the transfer, He didn't care what it said on the form V 317, neither what DVLC said. Within hours he was put firmly in his place by a DVLC official.

My project for the summer of 1983, was a cherished transfers survey. Using Car Numbers Monthly, I sent 7,000 questionnaires to people who are known to be interested in personalised registrations and included a reply paid envelope for each one. The operation cost a small fortune.

I was convinced that the public response to the 1981 Consultation Paper, would have proved conclusively to the Department of Transport, that a relaxation to the harsh transfer rules, was called for. However, the D.O.T., did not release any information, analysing the response, although they did claim for example, that there wasn't a demand for the return of the retention facility and that the ordinary motorist didn't want the opportunity to be able to transfer a number from a car to a motorcycle.

I spoke to the Policy Vehicles Section at DVLC and they seemed to be rather worried about my survey. After all, the results would most likely give me ammunition to fire at the Secretary of State for Transport and possibly expose DVLC for leading the Government "up the garden path".

At the time of going to press, the survey was only just beginning and only fifty or so replies had been received. The results proved as follows:-

41.8% said that the harsh transfer rules had persuaded them not to purchase a brand new car for at least twelve months. This result backed up my theory that the tortuous rules were costing the motor trade a fortune in lost sales and were actually affecting many thousands of British workers, who could have been benefiting from increased car sales and therefore increased work.

53.1% said that LVLO's attitude towards cherished transfers had improved over the past few years although 53.3% claimed that the service offered by LVLO's fell short of the high transfer fee being charged.

77.4% believed that DVLC, Swansea are basically against cherished transfers and 86.4% thought that there was too much red tape involved in transfers.

93.9% were not satisfied with the manner in which the 1981 Consultation was handled by the Dept. of Transport.

96.6% agreed that there should be no restriction of transfer between different classes of vehicles and 94.8% wanted the facility to be able to transfer from a car to a motorcycle.

93.2% wanted donor vehicle inspection reduced by at least 70%. This was a promise that had not been kept by the D.O.T. One of the requirements of donor vehicle inspection, is that it is to be taken to the LVLO by the applicant. 44.1% were prepared to pay an additional fee on top of the £80 transfer fee, to enable an official to visit their own premises to inspect the chasssis number on the donor vehicle. This result confirmed my theory that many jobs could be created within the civil service, to accommodate this demand.

The average cost of a cherished transfer, that would prove acceptable and justifiable, was, surprisingly, £38. I expected this to be lower.

It was hardly surprising that a large percentage (98.3%), wanted the retention facility returned.

Already DVLC have decided to hold back all prefix combinations between the numbers "1" and "20", presumably with a view to selling them at some time in the future.

The numbers game looks as though it will provide much interest for many years to come.

History

Ever since the 1903 Road Traffic Act received the Royal Assent, distinctive vehicle registration numbers have proved an attraction. From the 1st of January 1904, all motor vehicles were required by law, to be registered if they were to be used on the public highway.

The original cherished number is believed to be CA 1, although it was not the first cherished number to be transferred, it was originally reserved in September 1903 to the M.P., who guided the 1903 Road Traffic Act through Parliament. This Act which made registration numbers obligatory, received the Royal Assent earlier in the year, but the original registration letters were not allocated until the summer recess. Being a keen motorist, he wrote to the new registration officer in Denbigh, the area he represented, asking for the first number.

CA 1 was first transferred on the 5th July 1905. The reference to this transfer appears on page sixteen of the original register of numbers issued by Denbighshire County Council.

CA 1 was originally registered to an "Iris", further vehicles include a "White Steam Car" and a Sunbeam. In 1954 the number was transferred to a Riley RME, by the niece of the original owner. This car was spotted at a Canterbury hotel by Michael Stainer on the day before he took his Chartered Accountancy final in 1970. He established that the niece, who was a great age, would consider selling the car when she and her husband gave up driving, and accordingly sent them Christmas cards every year and postcards when on holiday. Six years later he had a phone call from the niece's sister-in-law, who related a sad tale; the niece's husband, now the only one who drove the car, was moving it to a new garage which had an awkward narrow entrance; unfortunately he got it wedged between the doorposts and was so upset at marking the car they kept in pristine condition for over 20 years, he had a heart attack and died.

Accordingly Michael Stainer was requested to remove the car forthwith, and when the sister-in-law came to see him at The Grand in Folkestone to arrange payment she was so taken with the suites he was renovating there she bought one of the largest ones.

About five years ago he acquired 111 RME from a Bentley T, which was more appropriate for a Riley RME, and accordingly CA 1 was transferred to its present car (seen with Mr. Stainer in the photograph) for a fee of £5 – the same fee its first transfer cost in Edwardian days!

Michael Stainer with his Rolls-Royce, CA1.

Original issues of registration numbers were not officially supposed to begin until 1st November 1903 and they did not have legal effect until 1st January 1904.

There was great interest at the time in acquiring distinctive short registrations, although the practise of linking one's initials with a registration, came approximately fifty years later. Also in 1903, Mr. Arthur Thring, First Parliamentary Counsel, who drafted the Registration Act, managed to acquire the first registration to be allocated in Somerset, Y1. The date was 12th November 1903, and a copy of the entry in the register of motor cars, is reproduced overleaf.

The first actual transfer of a registration number from one vehicle to another was on 3rd March 1904 when Dr. Robert Lauder of South-

Y1 Register and Y1 Original Car

ampton, transferred his number CR 1 from a 5 hp Kimberley car to an 11 hp Clement.

Many people wrongly assume that the first ever registration number was A 1. In fact, this was allocated in December 1903 to Earl Russell, a former Under Secretary for Air, who it is claimed, sat up all night, to be first in the queue for the number. Although, not the first number, A 1 could have been the most transferred registration number, up to the mid 1950's. By 1956 it had been transferred thirty seven times, and a few years later it was sold for £2,500. Such a high price was possibly assisted by considerable press coverage of this highly acclaimed registration number. It could also have been the press coverage that prompted Local Councils to meet a demand for distinctive registrations, by allocating numbers that were not currently in use, for the princely sum of £5. Such an example of a "give-away" number, was the allocation of M6 to Mr. Maurice Lord of Leicester, in 1959.

In 1962, the "giving away" of numbers was stopped. RR1 sold for £4,800 in 1968 at public tender. It was a world record price at the time and could set another world record if sold again.

Throughout the sixties, the public were becoming more and more aware of the existence of distinctive car registrations, however, it wasn't until the early seventies that the interest boomed.

In 1970-71 several enterprising people started to turn the buying and selling of registrations into full time business. Tim Sargent of Goudhurst, Kent (he owns TCS 1, TCS 1J, TCS 5 and TCS 303), claims to be the original number plate dealer, although he no longer trades in them. He purchased TCS 1 in 1969 and TCS 5 three years later.

In 1971, dealers were becoming established and it was decided to form an association. This was know as the P.N.D.A., (Personalised Numbers Dealers Association). Founder members included, David Kempson, Noel Woodall and John Atkins. By this time, there was no such thing as acquiring a number plate from a Local Council for £5, although this was to remain the fee payable for transferring a number from one vehicle to another.

Early P.N.D.A., meetings were often, quite heated affairs, with dealers having varying differences of opinion, however, it wasn't long before a code of practise was agreed and by 1973 it was a well established Association.

Between 1974 and 1976 the trading in registration numbers was booming. Many of the leading dealers were driving Rolls-Royces and enjoying a luxurious standard of living. However, by 1976 the job of registering and licensing motor vehicles had almost passed from Local Taxation Offices to the Driver and Vehicle Licensing Centre in Swansea. The centralisation of vehicle records meant that most registration number transfers were handled by DVLC, Swansea.

In July 1976 came the biggest shock in the history of cherished numbers. Civil Service

Unions objected to transferring numbers and without any warning, stopped all transfers. At first it was assumed that the strike wouldn't last long, however, several months passed by before the number dealers started to feel the pinch. A campaign office was set up in London, to co-ordinate a series of demonstrations and appeals on behalf of the public and trade alike. It wasn't until January 1977 that the Unions permitted transfers once again. However, the rules governing transfers were now far stricter and the fee was increased from £5 to £50. The Labour Government claimed "that it was right and proper that a good socialist profit should be made". Ironically no-one was objecting to the fee, after all, it made the owning of a distinctive registration, that much more difficult for the average motorist and therefore increased the status value of numbers.

The new transfer rules put some dealers out of business between 1977 and 1982, although private cherished number owners suffered the wrath of the transfer rules, and the majority proudly defeated the system and retained the rights to their number plates. The five years of conflict with the authorities, resulted in a considerable amount of national media coverage and coupled with extensive dealer advertising has led to the massive interest in distinctive registrations that exists today.

For those who are not fully conversant with the procedure of transferring a number from vehicle to vehicle, it should be explained that the actual number plates displayed on the car, are only worth the value of the metal or the perspex. It is the "rights" to the registration number that carries the value and those "rights" can be ascertained from supporting documentation, chiefly the vehicle registration document V5.

Stars and their Numbers

There was a time when people looked twice at every car with a distinctive registration, to see if the driver was a star of TV or films. This was before the numbers game became popular with commoners such as myself. These days, it is still an accepted tradition that the stars look for personalised registrations. I have sold quite a few numbers to personalities. The latest of which was comedian Charlie Daze, who visited my office on impulse. He was fascinated with personalised numbers. Three cups of coffee and a hundred jokes later, he settled for 7130 CD.

At the time of going to press, Britain's number one ladies' tennis player, Jo Durie, was interesed in acquiring one of my numbers (JOD 111E). Her interest in car numbers stemmed from reading my first book. She's not the only sporting personality interested in car numbers, Steve Ovett and Ray Reardon are amongst the others.

In March 1982, film star Norman Wisdom asked me to sell his personalised plate (1 NW), for him. He invited me to his London flat to discuss the sale. He and his charming wife Marion, made me most welcome and I spent a thoroughly enjoyable couple of hours with them. He didn't really want to sell the number, but as he now resides in the Isle of Man, where the number could not be used on a car, it was pointless keeping it in storage in London.

Magician, Paul Daniels once wrote to me asking if I could obtain MAG 1C for him., Unfortunately, he was out of luck, I couldn't conjure that one up for him, because it had never been issued.

It was rumoured in early 1983 that Jimmy Tarbuck was contemplating selling his classic number COM 1C (Comic), however, his agent has confirmed that the number is not for sale. Not that I am a good comic, but I must confess that I would have liked to own the number.

Some number plates have been credited to Stars through fictional links. For example 007 is associated with James Bond. It is in fact owned by a Mr. Tompkins from Edgware, Middlesex.

ST 1 (Simon Templar 1) is really owned by a London solicitor after being sold by Mrs. Gordon of Edinburgh from an old Austin Maxi, for the sum of £15,000.

WHO 1 has been used in the Dr. Who TV series, but is really owned by a gentleman in Hampshire.

Some American TV programmes use personalised plates in their series. Examples are Hart to Hart who have a series of HART numbers and the Fall Guy who uses the number FALL GUY.

The following pages detail some of the Stars and their numbers. If you know of any that are not listed here, please write to me at P.O. Box 1, Bradford-On-Avon, Wiltshire. The information will be used in the next edition of this book.

AA 10 *ANTHEA ASKEY*. actress, daughter of the late Arthur Askey. The number was inherited from her famous comedian father.

AAA 1 *THE MARQUIS OF EXETER*. Former Olympic Gold Medallist. President of the Amateur Athletic Association.

AFC 1 *ARSENAL FOOTBALL CLUB.* The number is used on Sir Guy Bracewell-Smith's car. He is the thirty year old football crazy Baronet.

AS 3921 *ANDY STEWART.* Scottish singer and dancer. He had a big hit with his single, "A Scottish Soldier".

ATV 1 *LEW GRADE.* Former director of ATV (now Central Television). His interests have included film making. He also owns LG 1.

BC 1 *BILLY COTTON JUNIOR.* This rare and valuable plate was owned by his famous bandleader father.

BFE 9 *BRUCE FORSYTH.* Born February 1928. Numerous television shows. He made his stage debut in 1942 at The Windmill Theatre.

BET 7 *VICTOR LOWNES.* of The Playboy club, fame.

BJM 1 *BERNARD MANNING.* Club and TV Comedian. Owner of the world famous, Embassy Club, Manchester. He is pictured here with his other distinctive and apt registration, 1 LAF. Also owns 11 LAF.

BMH 1 *BOB MONKHOUSE.* Born June 1929. Early TV shows include Candid Camera and The Golden Shot. Accomplished stage performer.

BR 8 *BRIAN RIX.* Now in semi-retirement. Best know for his leading roles in many farces for stage and television. He also owns BNR 1.

BS 1 *BILLY SMART (JUNIOR).* Circus master. BS 56, BS 57 & BS 58 are all in the family.

4 BSR *BARRY SHEENE.* Well known British motorcycle ace. The number is on his Rolls Royce Silver Shadow.

CCO 1 *COLIN CROMPTON.* Comedian. Well known as the compere of television's "Wheel-tappers & Shunters Club".

CD 455 *CHARLIE DRAKE.* Born June 1925. His real name is Charles Springall. Has been in television since 1950 with such shows as The Worker, Who is Sylvia & The Charlie Drake Show. He started in showbusiness as a club entertainer at the age of eleven.
He had a big success with his recording of "My Boomerang Won't Come Back".

7130 CD *CHARLIE DAZE.* Comedian. Featured in numerous TV programmes including ITV's "The Comedians". The number is on a Rover 3500.

CF 6915 *CLEMENT FREUD.* Born April 1924. Broadcaster, writer, caterer and Member of Parliament. He has even tried his hand at being a jockey. His other sporting interest is cricket and is a member of the Lords Taveners. He also owns the registration number UUU 3.

COM1C *JIMMY TARBUCK.* Born February 1940. Television includes Sunday Night At The London Palladium and Winner Takes All. He started in showbusiness by winning a talent contest at a Holiday Camp. Has been banned from driving. The registration, reading COM1 C is perhaps one of Britain's best known car number plates.

1 CUE *JIMMY WHITE.* Professional snooker player.

DC 1 *DAVE CLARK.* Sixties pop star and film star. Records include Bits & Pieces. Films include Catch Us If You Can.

DEC 707 *DEC CLUSKEY.* The younger of the Cluskey Brothers in the vastly popular group, The Bachelors. Hits include, "I Believe" and "Diane".

DLR 3 *DANNY LA RUE.* Born July 1926. Actor, Comedian & Female Impersonator. His real name is Daniel Patrick Carroll. He owns a night club in London and a hotel in Warwickshire

1 DLT *DAVE LEE TRAVIS.* Disc Jockey, with BBC Radio One. He has this number on a gigantic motorhome.

DS 5121 *DAVID STEEL.* Born March 1938. Leader of the Liberal Party since 1976. Former television interviewer for Scottish Television. Hobbies include angling and motoring. The number is on an Armstrong Siddeley.

ES 900 *ERIC SYKES.* Born May 1923. Comedian and script writer.

FAL 1 *FREDDY LAKER.* Born August 1922. Flamboyant director of Laker Airways from 1966 – 1982. Member of London's Eccentric Club. Knighted in 1978.

FAL 1C *JOHN ENTWISTLE.* Guitarist with the popular group "The Who". This number was previously owned by a Nottinghamshire schoolmaster.

FW 6 *FULKE WALWYN.* Well known race horse trainer. Based at Lambourn, Berkshire. Also owns FW 33.

GAG 22 *LENNIE BENNETT.* Comedian and television quiz master.

GER 1E *GERRY MARSDEN.* One of the sixties most famous pop stars, Gerry of Gerry & The Pacemakers. Hits include "How Do You Do It", "I Like It", "Ferry Cross The Mersey" and "You'll Never Walk Alone". The number is on a Daimler Sovereign.

GN 4 *GARY NUMAN.* Pop star and songwriter. Biggest hit to date, "CARS" Appropriately, the number plate is on a beautiful Ferrari. Hobbies include aviation.

HB 1000 *HUGH BEAN (CBE).* Born September 1929. Violinist. Leader of Philharmonic Orchestra 1957-1967. Has been a soloist with many leading orchestras. Associate leader BBC Symphony Orchestra for two years.

HS 92 *HARRY SECOMBE.* Born September 1921. Was once a clerk in a Steel Mill. Numerous T.V., since 1946. He has ten Royal Variety Performances to his credit. Knighted in 1981. Television and radio includes such extremes as

The Goons and Stars on Sunday. Photographed here with his Rolls-Royce Silver Shadow. He claims "92" was his waist measurement.

HW 6 *HOWARD WINSTONE.* Former featherweight champion of the world.

JM 1 *SIR JOHN MOORES.* President of the world famous "Littlewoods Organisation". The football pools firm is country's biggest. Also owns JM 2.

JR 6 *JOHN ROBERTS.* Roberts Brothers Circus. Also in the family, BR 30.

JS 954 *JIMMY SAVILLE.* Disc Jockey and TV personality. Began as a miner. His first involvement with showbusiness was managing a dance hall. He has raised millions of pounds for charity, including Stoke Mandeville Hospital, where he is a porter in his spare time. His numbers collection is completed with 1 EUS and PMJ 1 M.

KD 11 *KEN DODD.* Born November 1927. Many television shows to his credit. Hit records include "Happiness".

BC 29 *BARBARA CARTLAND.* Listed in the Guiness Book of Records, as the world's top selling author. She has written over 350 books and has sold an average of one million copies per book. In 1978 she sang an album of Love Songs with the Royal Philharmonic Orchestra. Her daughter Raiñe, married Earl Spencer in 1976.

KDT 1P *KARL DENVER TRIO.* Had a smash hit with the record "Whim Whe". The number is on a Granada and is driven by trio member, Kevin Neill. He wrote the "Harry Lime Theme".

KKA 1 *KEVIN KEEGAN.* International football star. Has captained England, Liverpool and Southampton, amongst others.

447 KM *KEVIN MABBUT.* Professional football player.

4 LAF *LENNY WINDSOR.* Comedian. TV series "The Comic Strip", Channel Four. The number is on a Rolls-Royce.

LDP 11 *LYNSEY DE PAUL.* Singer and songwriter.

3 LG *LARRY GRAYSON.* Comedian and television personality. Hosted BBC TV's "The Generation Game". Had one record (single) "Shut That Door", his catch phrase. Once owned the number plate GAY 33.

1 LPO *LONDON PHILHARMONIC ORCHESTRA.* World famous orchestra.

MCC 307 *COLIN COWDREY.* Former England Cricketer. He made 117 appearances for England, and was captain 23 times. When he retired in 1975, he held the record for most runs and most catches in Test Matches. CBE 1972. As well as the obvious link with MCC (Marylebone Cricket Club), his full name is Michael Colin Cowdrey.

600 MFK *GILBERT O'SULLIVAN.* Pop singer. Hits include: "Claire", "Whats In A Kiss" and "Get Down".

5727 MM *MARY MILLINGTON.* Star of glamour films.

MMM 1 *LORD MONTAGU OF BEAULIEU.* Born Oct. 1926. Author. Numerous television appearances. MMM stands for Montagu Motor Museum, which he founded in 1952 and four years later, he started the world's first motorcycle museum. In 1972 his museums became the National Motor Museum. Venue for several cherished registration rallies.

900 MPL *PAUL McCARTNEY.* McCartney Productions Ltd. Paul & Linda are directors. Former Beatles member and now Wings. World famous songwriter.

77 MW *JIM WATT.* Boxer. Former Light-Weight champion of the world.

NG 10 *NOELE GORDON.* Born December 1923. Television includes "Crossroads".

NDO 1 *NORTHERN DANCE ORCHESTRA.* They have orchestrated the perfect number.

OLE 8 *OLE OLSEN.* Three times, world speedway champion.

PAT 53 *PAT ROACH.* As Saturday afternoon TV addicts will know, he is one of the leading heavyweight professional wrestlers.

1914 PF *ARRIVAL.* Popular recording and cabaret group. Numerous TV appearances. As children they were known as "The Poole Family" and were seen regularly on Yorkshire TV's "Stars on Sunday" and "Junior Showtime". Their grandfather started in showbiz in 1914, when he formed a group called "The Bing Boys". Latest T.V., Starburst and 321.

PGA 1 *THE PGA.* Collectively owned by the Professional Golfers Association.

POP 1 *MITCH MURRAY.* Well known hit song writer. Married to actress and singer Grazine Frame, who owns GF 100.

PM 208 *PETE MURRAY.* Born September 1928. Actor and disc jockey. The 208 in the plate is relevant to his early days as a D.J., with Radio Luxembourg. Television includes Top Of The Pops and Juke Box Jury.

PR 1 *PETER ROWNTREE.* Chocolate manufacturing fame. Now a household name.

PR 11 *PAUL RAYMOND.* Flamboyant entrepreneur. London night club owner. The number is on a Rolls-Royce.

1 PRO *RAY REARDON.* Professional snooker player. Six times champion of the world.

PS 3429 *PETER SHILTON.* England Goalkeeper.

PUT 3 *PETER ALLIS.* Well known Golfer and TV commentator.

3 R *ROGER CLARK.* Famous rally car driver. He also owns, RY 3, RY 5, 1 BLO, 2 ANR.

RA 1 *RICHARD ATTENBOROUGH.* Born August 1923. Has starred in over fifty films.

RAK 7 *MICKIE MOST.* Sixties pop star and now record company director, RAK Records. Hence his RAK number plates. The collection is completed with RAK 9 and RAK 10.

RS 74 *BOB SHARPLES.* Band leader and television personality.

RW 100 *RICK WAKEMAN.* Pop star. Song writer. Also has the registration number HS 231.

SB 250 *STANLEY BLACK.* Orchestra leader. The number is on a Daimler Sovereign.

7 SEA *JIMMY CHIPPERFIELD.* Circus master and keeper of exotic wild animals.

SJO 100 *STEVE OVETT.* Olympic gold medalist. One of the country's top athletes.

SM 3 *SIR HECTOR MONRO MP.* Born October 1922 (Hector Seymour Peter Monro). Member of Parliament (Conservative) for Dumfries, since 1964. Also owns 3 SM and SM 4. Also in the family, SM 500 and HSM 1.

7 SOO *GRAHAME SOUNESS.* Liverpool football player.

SYD 126 *SID LITTLE.* The little half of comedy duo Little and Large. Television includes The Little & Large Show.

SYD 221 *SID LAWRENCE.* Band Leader, The Sid Lawrence Orchestra.

TOC 16 *TOM O'CONNOR.* Comedian. Host of ITV's popular programme "London Night Out" and well known for being quiz master of "Name That Tune". Also in the family AOC 100 and POC 133.

7 SM *STIRLING MOSS.* Stirling has been interested in car number plates for over twenty five years. The number "7" is particularly significant to him, as it was on Easter Monday, 1962 that his yellow Lotus, with his famous lucky number "7", went careering out of control at 140 mph, on the Goodwood race circuit. The accident left him unconscious for a month and he suffered paralysis for a further five months. Despite all this, he continued to regard the number "7" as lucky, hence, 7 SM, 777 SM, and SM 7.

TV 1 *BOB DANVERS-WALKER.* Born April 1907. Commentator and television announcer for such programmes as Wheel of Fortune and Take Your Pick.

UKE 1 *ALAN RANDALL.* George Formby impersonator. Plays the ukelele, hence UKE 1. Numerous television appearances including car numbers feature on Pebble Mill At One in 1978.

CB 78 *KATIE BOYLE.* (born 1929, Caterina Irene Helen Imperiali di Francavilla). Katie has hosted several Eurovision Song Contests and has many other TV credits. Her husband, Sir Peter Saunders (producer of London's longest running play, The Mousetrap), owns MOU 1 on a Rolls-Royce.

MB 1 *MAX BYGRAVES.* Born October 1922. Entertainer, Singer and Actor. Made his West End debut at The London Palladium in 1949. Has had many hit records. The number plate is on his Rolls-Royce.

VS 1234 *VICTOR SYLVESTER*. Owned by the famous band leader.

WFN 8 *RAY ELLINGTON*. Credited to the well known musician.

WTV 1 *PETER CADBURY*. Born Feb. 1918. Former director of ITN News Ltd and of Westward Television, (hence WTV).

WYN 1 *WYN CALVIN*. Welsh star of comedy. Known throughout Wales, as "The Prince of Laughter". The photograph shows Wyn with his wife Carole, at the Pier Pavilion, Llandudno. The registration number was given to him in 1960, in London, on the day it became due. It has been on fifteen cars since.

XP 1 *PETER LEPINO*. International Aerial Trapeze Artist. Billy Smart's Circus etc...

YOB 1 *SLADE*. Chart topping group for over ten years. Their records have sold many millions of copies all over the world. The registration, is on a gold Rolls-Royce.

Owners Gallery

This section is reserved for those people who want to be included in my pictorial reference to number owners. If you would like to be included in the next edition of this book, please send a good quality photograph, colour or black and white (preferably the latter), to Concise Guide, P.O. Box 1, Bradford-on-Avon, Wiltshire. A brief history would also be appreciated.

Budding photographers are also invited to take pictures of vehicles with interesting numbers as they travel around the country.

If your cherished number is not included in this book, please do not hesitate, get a picture taken, NOW.

A 1 – Owned for many years by the Dunlop Tyre Company of Birmingham. It is used on a Ford Granada Estate for publicity purposes.

A 470 – Mr. P.J. Newers of London. The car is a three seater 1904 Star.

AA 1 – is currently on the Automobile Association's 1904 Renault Park Phaeton, and AA 2

adorns one of a collection of old motor cycles, a 1922 2½ hp solo Chater Lea.

These numbers were the first to be issued by the old Hampshire County Licensing Office and were acquired by the Association in the 1950s. Initially they were both attached to Chater Lea motor cycles representative of those used by AA patrols in the 1920s.

The 1904 Renault is typical of the vehicles which would have been on Britain's roads when the Automobile Association was founded in 1905. It was felt appropriate to transfer the AA 1 registration number to this vehicle, especially as it regularly competed in veteran car rallies and in the annual London to Brighton run.

AA 11 – 1903 Daimler, National Motor Museum at Beaulieu.

AA 16 – The Montagu collection, Beaulieu. This car was the first to enter the yard of the House of Commons. It is an 1899 Daimler 12hp.

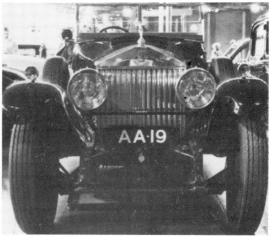

AA 19 – 1925 Rolls Royce Phantom at the National Motor Museum.

AA 20 – 1903 De Dion Bouton at the National Motor Museum.

65 AAB (6 SAAB) – On a Saab Turbo, owned by Mr. R. Bishop of Birmingham.

1 **AAO** – Owned by Councillor Westall, Cumberland.

1 **AAT** – John Barman of Scarborough, North Yorkshire.

7 **ADD** – Appropriately owned by the Managing Director of Severn Advertising, of Kidderminster, Worcestershire. This is another example of unorthodox style lettering on the plate. There are no regulations actually stipulating the style of characters.

10 **AFJ** – Alan Justice, Northwich, Cheshire.

AGH 96 – Dr. Alfred Gordon Hooker, Ludlow, Shropshire.

AJT 222 – Mr. and Mrs. Shilling of London. Many will recall Mrs. Shilling's KGC 12D

number plate, that graced her Rolls-Royce Silver Cloud III (a magnificent car, once the property of Lord Derby).

Unfortunately, she sold the car during the 1976 Civil Service strike and lost her treasured number plate. However, she is open to any offers of number plates that include the 12D, for "Shilling".

Luckily, her current Rolls-Royce carries a distinctive registration, AJT 222. At first glance it may not look much, until you learn that it is extremely rare, as the AJT combination was issued only once in 1939 (with the exception of suffixes). The licensing authority was Dorset.

named his house after his registration number. He lives at Ambi Cottage.

6 AKJ 1957 Volkswagen mini bus owned by Mr. E. J. Wegener, Hertfordshire.

ALF 1 & 1.ALF – Alf Page of Ascot. First in class, at the Longleat numbers rally 1982.

AR 2 – 1898 Daimler at Beaulieu Motor Museum.

AMB 1 – A winner of several rally prizes for Mr. A. M. Battye of Crossland Moor, Huddersfield, Yorkshire. The initials are also the same for his wife. Mr. Battye may have started a trend, he has

ASH 752 & ASH 460 – Jill and Colin Ash from Guildford. ASH 460 has been in the family since

1971. ASH 752 was only transferred after the donor vehicle was restored at some expense.

7737 AW – Anthony Whitear of Purley, Surrey. The number was purchased in August 1982 and is on a 1976 Mercedes 280 SE.

AWE 6 – Steven McVitie of Ripon, North Yorkshire, has this rare 1934 Sheffield registration, on his Jaguar.

AXS 1 – Owned by "IT'S A SECRET" mobile discotheque, based in Ayr, Scotland.

B 2 – Barry Thomas of Coventry. Former registration number dealer and founder member of the Personalised Numbers Dealers Association (now the C.N.D.A.). He left the business to start a recording studio and had a degree of success with the advent of "Ska Music" in the late seventies.

2 BAD Trevor Waite of Wilton, owns "too bad and bad two, too".

BEN5ON – The priceless property of David Benson from Wetherby, Yorkshire.

3150 BH – Brian Henthorne of Corsham, Wiltshire. The registration number also incorporates his telephone number.

BLP 999 – 1934 Lancia Augusta at the National Motor Museum.

9 BOB – Bob Gilbraith of Leeds

BOO 8 (BOOB and supporting collection) – John Atkins of Chessington. Possibly the largest set of numbers of a similar appearance. The others (all

registered to vehicles) are:- A 800, BOO 13, 800 BY, 80 OBY, BOO 800, 800 BOO, BOO 800B, BOO 888B and 000 800D.

1 BOT – John Buckwell, Ilford, Essex.

23 BOX & 45 BOX – Mr. & Mrs. John Elford-Box of Rotherham, Yorkshire.

9549 BP Bruce Pyne, Bedford. Displayed on a Ford Cortina.

BRA5IL – owned by Mr. M. Jones of Thirsk (also owns TCP 18). He spotted it on a garage forecourt and bought it as a runabout. It is quite likely that this is one of the rare occasions when a car dealer has sold a vehicle for less than the true value, without realising it, as he had no idea of the significance of the registration number (although he does now). The Brazilian Embassy were not interested in buying the plate. They already have BRA 1 and BRA 2.

BRE 1 D – (Spaced out as B REID), for Bill Reid of Edinburgh.

BRU5 H (Brush) – The perfect registration mark for painter and decorator, John Hillman from Cardiff. He also owns GLO 552 (Gloss 2)

BS 35 – Mr. & Mrs. B. Simmonds of Reading. Displayed on a 1981 Vauxhall.

1 BTR – Mr. & Mrs. G. Stafford of Romsey, Hampshire.

BUN 1 – Mr. D. Graham, Newport, Gwent. Managing director of a bakery firm.

BV 7 – Mr. & Mrs. Oliver Hacking of Virginia Water, Surrey. This was the seventh number to be issued in Blackburn and was originally owned by the Hacking family.

616 CAM – Allan Cameron Campbell, Old Roan, Liverpool.

CB 26 – Clive Boorman of Sittingbourne, Kent. Clive is a professional photographer and uses his registration number in his business title, "CB 26 FOTOS". The registration was first issued to Hugh Mellor of Blackburn in 1904.

7 CCV – Property developer, Mark Henwood, of Wadebridge, Cornwall, pictured here at the 1977 Rally at Dodington. CCV is the name of his Company and he claims that 7 is his lucky number.

CEB 2 – Mr. & Mrs. C. E. Broadbent & Family from Coventry.

CHR 151 (Chris 1) – Chris Dyke of Luton, Bedfordshire.

6 CJB – Christopher J. Baldwin, Eastleigh, Hampshire. Former dealer in cherished numbers.

CLASSY – John Field of Hayes, Middlesex. The authorities obviously missed the significance of this "classy" number. It was issued through North West London, LVLO in October 1982.

1 CLT – On a bus, owned by London Transport.

11 & 22 COE My father bought me 11 COE as a 21st birthday present in 1971. He paid £30. Since then it has been on about 8 cars and is currently on my Rover 3500. Imagine my surprise, when I was idly looking at number plate advertisements when I spotted 22 COE for sale. At the time my wife was in the process of selling her car so we didn't have a car to put it on. The problem was solved by buying the donor vehicle. the number pictured, is now on my wife's Mini Metro. Strangely enough, COE is not an unusual number in our area (near Croydon). An Insurance Broker who lives a mile away owns 1 COE and 2 COE and I occasionally see a Morris Minor number 19 COE. The big question is however– where is 33 COE? Peter Coe

1 COW – Many people link their number plates with their names/businesses/cars etc... Carol Moore of Wentworth, Surrey, assures me that her number plate is not linked to her personality. The car is decorated with a set of horns and other cow goodies, Good job her name isn't Pat !

CT 44 – Cecil Thompson of County Durham, bought this number in 1972 when he was 44. It cost £160 and has considerably increased in value since.

CT 50 – Grahame Calvert-Thomson of Southport, Merseyside.

471 CWC – Charles W. Cayzer, Charlbury, Oxford.

2 CWT – Kath Withers, Winsford, Cheshire.

1 CYO – Colin Youle, London SW4.

3 D – This superb fun number would look far better on a 3 D perspex plate. Owned since July 1964, by Mr. R. J. Cruttenden of Kent.

9 D – Jack Henley, Transport Contractor and Farmer. He lives in Goudhurst, Kent. He also owns JRH 5, 12 D, 300 D, HN 77 and WNW 7.

D 25 Mr. R. P. Jeffs of Bromley, has owned this number for twenty-five years.

44 D – Mr. Bakewell of Oxford, on a BMW 525

60 D (GOD) – This almighty plate, is owned by Mr. Orrin of Chigwell, Essex.

55 DAF – The combination of 55 DAF on a DAF 55 car, has won several prizes at rallies, for owner, Michael Chilcott of Somerset.

DC 10 – David Cooper, Melksham, Wiltshire. The number is on a Jaguar XJS. One day, when

43

the car was parked at Heathrow airport, a stewardess left a note on the car, asking him if he was a DC 10 pilot and if he would telephone her. David is in fact the owner of a frozen food store.

5 DCY – Stavros Galanos, Swansea. Obtained on 15th August 1962, with a brand new, Vauxhall VX 490, and has been transferred from car to car ever since. The letters "DCY" have no significance, it is purely kept for sentimental reasons. Stavros is rather unlucky that the Government have cashed in on cherished transfers, as the increased transfer fees, make it an expensive hobby.

DEK 1 – Dave Kendall, specialist motor vehicle repairer from Bristol.

61 DER-CIDER. Owned by H. P. Bulmers Ltd. Pictured here with John Bishop, chauffeur to Bulmers' boss, Peter Prior.

61 DGH – David G. Humphreys of Kelvedon, Essex. Purchased in 1976 just before the Civil Servants' strike. Unfortunately, the dispute meant that the number could not be transferred from the vehicle and as the situation dictated, David was forced to sell the car. However the next owner agreed to let him transfer the number at a later date. Two years later the transfer was completed to a mini van and in 1983 the number was transferred again to a Metro.

4200 DH – David Hanson, Poynton, Cheshire. Sons, Mark and Craig are in the photograph.

DK 19 – Mr. D. Krite, London E2. Pictured here in the London rush hour traffic.

505 DK – David Knight, Senior Administrator at the National Motor Museum, Beaulieu, Hampshire.

DL 1 – This number plate is truly cherished, by Mr. & Mrs. P. S. Whaley of Bournemouth. The number was purchased over fifty years ago, by Mr. Whaley's father. It has remained in the family ever since.

DOD 34 – Alan Pettit of Trowbridge. Photographed here with his daughter, Tanya. This old Devon registration was found on a 1939 Austin Lorry.

DON 642 – 1937 Wolseley 25. Once owned by Lord Nuffield. Now on display at the National Motor Museum.

DVO 1 – Bruce Moss, Bradford, Yorkshire.

DWW 111 – David W. Withers of Cleveland. On a Rolls-Royce Silver Cloud III.

E 3 – Lucy Morton, Rugby, Warwickshire.

E 53 – Rob Walker of Frome, Somerset.

EAF – The EAF series photographed, belongs to Mr. E. A. Fishburn of Wetherby, Yorkshire. His interest in car numbers started in 1972 and by

1981 his collection of EAF plates had risen to four. He has won three 1st prizes at R.N.C. rallies.

When he started a business, selling car parts, he called it Express Auto Factors, specifically to coincide with his initials. This has now given his car numbers collection even more relevance

EEE 333 – Whether you look at this in the rear view mirror or the right way around, it will always be EEE 333. The style of lettering has been cleverly chosen by Mr. B. G. Redman of Newport, Gwent.

EEL 5 – Or Eels. F. Cooke & Sons of London, (established 1862). After many years of searching, this perfect registration number wasn't as slippery as their wares. The van can be found at car number rallies, selling hot or jellied eels.

EFL 1 and EFL 2 – Fred and Denise Leigh of Crewe, Cheshire. Also in the family, EFL 3 and FL 3. Being a Police Officer, Fred comes into daily contact with vehicle registration numbers. His own collection was started over ten years ago and he travels many hundreds of miles, to attend the rallies.

3 EJB – Edward J. Brady, Numberplan Insurance, Melksham, Wiltshire. The photograph includes son, Robbie, who has a few years to wait, to drive the family Rolls-Royce 1 LKX.

1 EMR Mr. & Mrs. G. V. Hancock of Trowbridge, Wiltshire. The significance of the number is that it remains in the county of origin, having been transferred several times by Mr. Hancock.

33 EJB – 1963 Mini Cooper at the National Motor Museum, owned by B.L. Heritage.

6 EOF (GEOF) – Geoff Pritchard of Warrington, Cheshire.

ER2 – You can be excused for thinking that ER2 has a connection with royalty. In fact, it belongs to Andrew Rabaiotti from Penarth, who enjoys a regal pretence.

13 ERT (BERT) – Bert Lokert of Oxford. Attends many rallies with his unusual Stimson three-wheeler.

EW 1 – Mrs. E. Wells, of Wakefield, West Yorkshire. Husband owns HW 1.

5 EXE – Robert Knierem, Billericay, Essex. He claims that his wife gets some extraordinary looks, when driving!

350 F – Francis Evans, Penarth, South Wales.

FJ 18 – The cherished property of Mr. S. R.

48

Shepherd, from Dawlish, Devon. This number was originally allocated to a 1912 Wolseley, owned by Mr. Shepherd's father. The car was broken up in 1938 to make space for workshop extensions. Although, the registration mark was retained, and has been on ten different vehicles, prior to the present Alfa Romeo.

FJT 1– Jointly owned by Mrs. A. Shoosmith and Mrs. G. M. Nash and kept at Beaulieu Museum.

2 FRY – Quite an apt registration, for Mr. T. Gordon Berry of Freckleton, Lancashire. He trades as "Berrigood Ham" and is also in the take away food business.

1 FTT – Mr. M. Allan from Clitheroe, Lancashire. This registration number is still on the original 1960, Triumph Herald.

20 FUS – Spaced to read "2 OF US". Purchased in September 1982 from singer songwriter, Tony Hatch, by Peter Baynham of Multilink Promotions, East Grinstead, Surrey. The number is now on a Rolls-Royce Silver Shadow.

FXG 1– Mr. A. Auton of Leeds, Yorkshire.

G 17 – This rare Glasgow number has found its way south of the border and now lives at Preston. The owner is Mr. J. Malcolm.

28 GAR – Gary Williams, Newport, Gwent. Also matches the 2.8 Ford Granada.

GBR 170N – John Hetherington of Northmberland, entered his patriotic number plate GBR 170N (G. Briton), in the 1977 Registration Numbers Club Rally, complete with a Datsun.

As many people commented about the car not being British, he had little choice, but to sell the Datsun and buy a British car. He settled for a Vauxhall Chevette and promptly transferred the registration number to it.

Since retiring in 1980, John has had a few tempting offers but he says, "it would take an offer in four figures before I finally part company with the loyal plate."

GD 1 George Dowty of Cheltenham, has owned this classic number since 1975.

GEE 47 – is on my Vanden Plas 1300, the number has been in the family for many years. The car number appeared at the first Car Numbers Rally held at Woburn Abbey in September 1973 and I have taken it to nearly all of the Rallies since then which have been held at Beaulieu, Dodington and Woburn Abbey.

In April 1976 The Car Number won 3rd prize Class 4 at Beaulieu.

GEE 144, was only obtained last year for my brother's car, a Cortina Ghia. In 1981 we took both cars to Dodington. We are one of the few people who can get their entire surname on their number plate.

Stephen & Clifford GEE,
Hampstead London.

50

GGM 1 – Mr. G. G. Middleton of Tadcaster, Yorkshire.

100 GLE – Displayed on an Audi GLE by Ray Bristow of London.

5 GMO – Mr. J. A. Naive of London. The number has been transferred to his 1904 Cadillac.

GOO 5H – Brian Rutland-Stow of Solihull, West Midlands, has spent over £4000 customising this 1976 Triumph Stag. He decided to purchase the fun number "GOOSH" in 1981, prior to the car's appearance at the Custom Car Show.

GT 200 – The Lloyd family of New Milton, Hampshire. The number was transferred from an old motorcycle. The Audi provides a much better home for the plate.

H 3 – Brian Heaton, Southport, Lancashire. Member of the Registration Numbers Club and organiser of the Southport number rallies.

GUN 181 – David Hare, New Malden, Surrey. The number is relevant to David's hobby of shooting and causes much amusement with the association of "GUN" and his surname "HARE".

9200 LJ & JJJ 55 – Porsche 911 SC, and Panther Lima respectively. Owned by Leslie and Margaret Jones of Reigate, Surrey.

H 1864 – National Motor Museum. 1904 Siddeley.

HEW 5ON (HEWSON) – John Hewson, of Harrogate, Yorkshire. Member of the Registration Numbers Club.

HJE 43 – Haydn Edwards, Salisbury, Wiltshire.

20 HJF – was spotted some 9 years ago doing 50 mph in the slow lane of the M1 in Leicestershire (its native habitat!) I drove past (mind in neutral) only to realise some two miles or so further on what I had seen. I slowed to 40 mph and eventually 20 HJF on a rather tired Hillman Minx overtook me and I duly followed. Happily it turned off at the next junction and I managed to stop the somewhat bemused owner. Eventually after a midnight telephone call some six months later, and a train journey the Hillman was mine. My next door neighbour's wife fell in love with the car and the net cost of 20 HJF was £20! – an apt sum! Howard Frazer, Dunstable.

HMD 1K – Mr. & Mrs. H. McDermid of Bath, Avon. They used to own 1 HMD but have settled for the alternative to grace their Porsche.

HMJ 100 – 1935 Chrysler at the National Motor Museum.

HOP 1N – The Opel Centre, Leek, Staffordshire. The perfect number for a demonstration car.

545 HOT – Finding an "AH" registration

number can be difficult and costly, as Andrew Hayton of Clarkston, Glasgow, discovered.

Unfortunately for Andrew, he has two of the most popular name initials. Hence there is a big demand for them and consequently, asking prices are high.

The alternative to initials, is a number plate that will suit the car. Andrew found 545 HOT advertised and after a little haggling with a fellow Scot, a price was agreed.

Andrew is overjoyed with the finished product. It has given his BMW 323I, a new dimension.

HOT 900 – Mr. Lee of Harrogate, Yorkshire. Displayed on an immaculate Ferrari. Also owns LEE 77 on another Ferrari.

HOW 1 – Peter How, The How Group of Companies, Edgbaston, Birmingham.

HT 4 – owned since 1974 by Edward Dowty from Cheltenham, Gloucestershire.

HU11 – Mrs. Marlene Kitchen not only has the distiction of being a director of the well known Hull car firm, "Arncliffes". She proudly drives Hull's most unique registration number (HU11), on a Mercedes 230 CE.

HW 1 – H. Wells of Wakefield, West Yorkshire. Wife owns EW 1.

55 JAC – Mr & Mrs V. Perrior of Torrington, North Devon. The number was inherited with the car.

JAC769 – Owned by NVT Motorcycles Ltd and on display at Beaulieu.

JAG 143 – Displayed as JAG 1 4.3 on a 1965 Mk 1 E Type Jaguar, by Forbes Robertson of Ayr.

JB 34 – First issued in 1932, Mr. J. Bentall of Ripon, Yorkshire, has acquired a potentially valuable family asset. Not only is the registration rare, but the initials JB are one of the most sought after combinations.

JB 1850 – J. Bernstein, London.

JBW 11 – The photograph above shows John Watts of Earls Barton, Northamptonshire, with part of his number plate collection.

The number came from a 1955 Rover, PMW 666 from a 1967 Austin and GJW 12 from an old banger dating back to 1948.

The latter plate was purchased by John (at an undisclosed price), for son Graham.

The family interest in personal number plates started from the hobby of spotting distinctive registrations. The collection took almost ten years to complete.

As well as being a member of the Registration Numbers Club, John is also a member of the Volvo Club.

JCC 9 – Mr. J. C. Crane of Mudeford, Dorset.

JD 59 – John Darlington, Moseley, Birmingham. Also couples as his business name, (J.D. Electrical). Apart from the increased value (which John claims is just a bonus), the number has given him much pleasure.

JEA 50N – Crafty spacing, makes this seemingly insignificant registration, a priceless gem for John Eason of Banstead, Surrey.

JEE 24 – The number was bought in 1976 as a present for my wife's 24th birthday. I held the number from June until August so I could put the number on to a new car, unfortunately in July 1976 the civil service unions began their ban on processing cherished marks, but by some miracle my new car was registered with JEE 24 on the 1.8.76.

I have turned down an offer of £750 for my plate, not bad for an investment five years ago of £175, but no amount of money would secure it now. From being a very small boy spending my summer holidays sitting by the roadside day after day collecting car reg. numbers it has always been my ambitions to own my own plate. It also helps when the plate contains your full surname as mine does – KEN GEE.

JES 5 – Cleverly displayed by Jess Childs of Luton, to look like JESS.

JK 1974 – Mr. M. Mullihill of Birmingham.

JL 66 – I bought the number in August 1980, and received the tax disc only the day before attend-

ing the rally at Newby Hall on Sunday, 7th September. The number is at present on an orange Cortina MkIII, which I consider to be only a temporary car, as it will be in my father's name from the end of 1981, while I shall be saving hard for a better class of car, hopefully a Jensen Interceptor.

Ever since the early 1970's, when I first became aware of the existence of personal number plates, I was determined to own my own number plate. You can imagine my delight on that September day last year, when I realised my ambition. Furthermore, I'll consider it a really special day, the day I'll be able to transfer the number onto what I consider to be my 'dream' car, namely a Jensen.

Unfortunately, I do not know its history, except that it was issued in 1932 by the Boston L.V.L.O. Any help in tracing its history will be most welcome.

Jason Latham
Swansea

JS 360 – James Smith from Cheltenham, Gloucestershire. His son, Robin, owns RS 778.

JS 9374 – John Straw of Mickleover, Derbyshire, purchased this registration number in January 1983 and had it transferred to his Volvo 244. His wife, Jill, was more amicable than many wives are, when their husband tells them that they have decided to spend several hundred pounds on a personalised registration number for the family car, she shares the same initials. John is a professional wildlife and landscape artist.

57 JOE – Joe Gaskin. Middlesborough night club owner. He also owns JOE 57.

JP 4 – This number has been owned for over thirty years by John Perkins of Harrogate. Class 4 winner at the Registration Numbers Club Rally, in 1978.

3 JYC – Owned by John and Jane Rabbits from Bath.

58

5050 K and 5511 K – Rob Ketley of Mold, Clwyd.

5 KAE – Ken Elliott, Cheltenham, Gloucestershire.

KFR 1 – Knight Frank and Rutley, Estate Agents, London.

999 KOP – Mr. D. Sulley, Mansfield, Nottinghamshire.

7898 KR – The owner wishes to remain anonymous but has submitted the story of her husband's (Mr. R.) dramatic experience when attempting to transfer the number plate on her behalf.

59

The story starts at 9.00 a.m. on Friday, 29th May, 1981. Mr. R. transports via trailer, an Austin Mini car which he purchased just over three months previously from a registration number dealer. The vehicle was not roadworthy but it was M.O.T.'d for approximately a further four weeks. He had purchased the whole car as he wanted to use the Mini after the transfer. The dealer had offered to carry out the transfer himself; however, Mr. R. decided to do it alone.

At 9.45 a.m. Mr. R., and his five year old son, arrive with the Mini, (the donor vehicle) outside the Local Vehicle Licensing Office in Colston Street, Bristol. Mr. R., presented the documents to the inspecting officer, whom he terms as a "jean clad civil servant", who was then accompanied by a similarly attired civil servant, and the pair of them proceeded to inspect the Mini. Now – unbeknown to Mr. R., his good lady, a model housewife, who had been keeping the papers of the Mini, "safely", in the kitchen window sill, noticed that the sunlight had faded the writing on the M.O.T. certificate. She then proceeded to write over the details in fresh ink. However, she incorrectly re-wrote July instead of June as the expiry date. (Although of course if should be noted that the M.O.T. was current in any case.) Coupled with this "blunder", the insurance certificate had been amended by the insurance agent, whereas the agent should have issued a new certificate, instead of writing over his error. Mr. R., followed the zealous civil servants back into the Licensing Office and one of them asked Mr. R. to step inside a small office. After a ten minute wait with no explanations, Mr. R. sensed that something was wrong and he expected the Manager to appear at any moment. Meanwhile, he could see the "jean clad pair", frantically telephoning.

At 10.30 am, two burly Police Officers from the Avon Constabulary, entered the office and informed Mr. R. that they had been summoned to arrest him. Mr. R. was then formally arrested and accompanied by the Police Officers out of the office, through the public foyer, into the busy centre street where a further Police Officer assisted Mr. R. and five year old son into a Panda car. A further bevy of Police Officers were swarming around the Mini, which was being impounded. The car was escorted from the scene by a Constabulary Squad car and together with the Panda car, and flashing lights, they left the scene amidst bustling onlookers, including the civil servants.

At 11.45 a.m. Mr, R. and son were released from the Central Police Station. The documents had been checked out and the explanations accepted, with a degree of unspoken sympathy. The two amiable arresting officers advised Mr. R. to apply for a duplicate M.O.T. certificate and to arrange for the vehicle to be taken back out of the Police compound. It was obvious now, that the bureaucratic civil servants had over-reacted by dialling "999" in the first place. They later claimed that they were unable to get through to the Police on any of the sixteen normal lines, and in desperation, made an emergency 999 call.

Mr. R's traumatic experience left an unanswered question. Why didn't the Manager or another senior civil servant, question the amended papers before calling the Police? Why were the LVLO staff showing a degree of resentment towards his cherished transfer application from the word "go".

The conclusion drawn is that whilst it cannot be denied that Mrs. R. should not have written over the faded M.O.T. certificate, the Licensing Office should have given Mr. R. the chance to explain what had happened and his explanation could have been easily checked out and pending this enquiry the transfer application should have been held. The Civil Servants caused Mr. R and family extreme embarassment and considerable worry over a simple transaction that the Department of Transport had the audacity to charge £50 for the SERVICE! The number was transferred by Bristol L.V.L.O. two weeks later.

KSN 1L – Mr. & Mrs. K. Sellers of Barnet, Hertfordshire. Also in the family, PS 3424.

LC 7777 – Mr. M. Edwards of London. The car is a 1904 Hotchkiss.

55 LEA – Richard and John Lea from Clwyd, North Wales, pictured at the 1982 Longleat Numbers Rally.

LEO 15 – I got talking to a lad riding a moped, who had pulled up at traffic lights, in Bayswater Road, London. His registration number was LEO 15, simply couldn't resist asking him whether he would consider selling it! His reply was, "I love my bike dearly but would take £40 for it." It was a deal and he delivered the bike with log book etc. the same evening. The morning after the transfer had been duly effected, the bike was pinched, that was the last I heard of it! Leo Landseer – London.

LES 24 – Les Graham of Leeds. Pictured here, collecting his prize at the 1979 Harewood Rally, for a low or neat registration, relevant to the owner.

LES 850 – Les Aris of Aylesbury, Buckinghamshire.

LLR 1 – L. L. Robinson, building contractor from Harrogate, Yorkshire. Also in the family, LRO 6.

LNX 1 & 999 LNX – The Lynex family, Robert, David and Denise, purchased LNX 1 in 1975. It was originally issued to an agricultural tractor in 1951. It has since been transferred to three MGB GT's. Unfortunately, 1 LNX is proving elusive. The owner is adamant that he will never part company with it. However, possibly the next best thing is 999 LNX. The Lynex's now have the first and the last LNX combinations to be issued without year letters.

LHC 17 – Mr. L. H. Coulthard of Bath, Avon.

2457 LJ – I thought you might like to see the photograph of my A35 Van. It might appear to be just an older vehicle with an ordinary number but in fact it was an 'E' registration until I purchased the LJ (for Lesley-Jane) number. I couldn't afford my full initials of LJB but had to settle for LJ. It caused some comments when the transfer was made as they said they usually transferred numbers from A35's rather than to an A35!

Miss Lesley Burgess, Cowplain, Hampshire.

LOB 797 – National Motor Museum, Beaulieu. On a 1950 "AC".

5 LOO and LOO 6 – Mr. & Mrs. Lewis Ball, of Potters Bar, Hertfordshire, The former has been in the family since 1975 and the latter since 1980. Either number could be well suited to a Rolls!

2 LRR – First issued in Nottingham for a Beetle Volkswagen 4 seater private car.

After 10 years' use, the car was placed in a garage at Nottingham, the owner advertising its sale in the treasured registration number column of Car Weekly.

It was at this time my son Lloyd was looking for a temporary vehicle to compensate for the loss of our Scimitar which burnt out on the M1 Motorway.

Browsing through the adverts he noticed his initials on the car description detail. He also took note of the cost and it was both these points he discussed to persuade my wife Pat and I to agree to become the new owners. We liked the idea and promptly travelled to Nottingham, had a test run and drove it back to Barnet.

The car was used for about 12 months in my building business in London before we decided to obtain a replacement vehicle.

2 LRR was then transferred to a Range Rover as shown in photograph.

Three years later we decided to dispense with the Range Rover but oh no not the registration number. Transfer arrangements once again put into effect and the Citroen Estate in the photograph became the mechanical display piece. The Citroen has almost had its day now but oh no not the registered number. Transfer arrangements are once again being prepared and as we decided against selling our Range Rover 2 LRR will once again be displayed for the second time round.

Now that the chequered history of this treasured number is in print is there another number in current circulation which can match the number of transfers and to be reinstated for the second time on a vehicle? We think it will take some beating.

– The Reynolds Family, Barnet.

M 111 – A conveniently placed bolt, on the first "1" turns M 111 into Mill for Mill Garages of Stockton-on-Tees, Clevland.

M 123 – Mrs. Martin of Houndsditch.

M 127 – Mr. F. J. Tipton of Ludlow, Shropshire. When he joined the Metropolitian Police in 1954, Mr Tipton was given a divisional number M 127. Southwark Police Station was the headquarters of "M" Division at the time, it was possible to buy numbers from the relevant local authority if it was not in use, for the princely sum of £5. Mr. Tipton's luck was in, and he happily paid the fee and had the number transferred to a motorcycle. Many transfers later, the machine carrying the plate is pictured. Also in his motorcycle collection are DS 4976, GJ 4362 and FO 6400.

MAG 11G and MAG 123 – Magician, Brian Miller of Ilford, Essex, had been looking for a personalised plate for several years. After discovering that MAG 1C had never been issued, he settled for a MAG 123. Brian is a member of the Magic Circle.

Fellow magician, Anthony J. Shelley has MAG 11G on his Citroen. He was once offered MAG 1G at £10,000, however, at that inflated price, he decided to give it a miss.

MAG 687 – Maggie Hankinson, Ross-onWye, Herefordshire. After rebuilding the Series 2 E Type Roadster in 1976, husband Barry, found the registration number to add the finishing touch.

MCA 74 – Andrew McAlpine, London SW3. Some time ago the company of Sir Robert

McAlpine & Sons Ltd., had a number of these plates ranging from MCA 1 to MCA 999. A few still remain and like MCA 74 is on the car of a member of the McAlpine family. The car is a limited edition Porsche 924 Carrera GT.

MCA 495 – Sara McAlpine, Oxford. Another of the McAlpine family collection.

MCH 26 and MCH 260. I started my numbers collection with MCH 260 which was acquired in July 1980, when I purchased a James 150cc motor cylce with a Villiers engine, first registered in 1958.

In February 1982, I was able to complete the set when I purchased a Mobylette, two wheeled moped, first registered in 1958.

The letters refer to my full name and by sheer coincidence, number 8 happens to be my lucky number. Michael C. Heaton, Bingley, West Yorkshire.

MEN 15 – F. Cooke & Sons, London.

MF 72 – Mervyn Fine writes: MF 72 was issued to me by Leicester County Borough Council in the late 50's or early 60's just before the reissue of dead numbers was stopped. I used it on successive motor cycles of mine until in 1973 I "bought" my allocated company car for a few days and transferred the number to that car when I "bought" it. That incidentally, was the Triumph P1 which is now MF 72.

In 1962, when I was due for a new company car, my employer transferred MJF 72 from my old company car to my new company car, and sold me my old one for its written down value. The new company car was the Triumph 2500S which still bears the number, though in 1979 when I was issued with my present company car (which bears a very mundane number) I bought the second Triumph.

Meanwhile, some time round late 1974 or early 1975 I saw the number MF 72 advertised in the Sunday Times. It was obviously meant for me, but I was not particularly flush at the time and did not put in the highest bid. A year later I saw the same number advertised in the same newspaper and I knew that it was meant for me. Again I did not put in the highest bid, but this time the chap who did overbid me mucked the advertiser about so much that I had a phone call a few weeks later offering me the number at the price I had bid.

So I sold my motorbike to the advertiser and then bought it back from him, by which time it was registered as MF 72, and I put on it a pair of my old MJF 72 motorcycle plates with the J blanked out, white at the front and yellow at the rear. This attracted the attention of the local police, who were not used to 1974 motor cycles with 1923 registrations.

My normal method of travelling to work for over 36 years has been by motorbike (17½ miles each way now) and I had been stopped by the police for having MJF 72 without suffix on what was obviously a much newer machine. However, I survived.

The third car, the Wolseley Hornet, I bought new in 1967. The day before I took delivery, I telephoned Leicester County Borough Council and asked them what chance there was of getting MJF 72F issued to me, and how long I should have to wait before registering my new car. Their answer was that I could have it the next day, so I did, and I've still got it – the same one-owner box of rust, held together with paint.

The only loose end in this story is the transfer of MF 72 from my motorbike to the Triumph PI. I managed that by the skin of my teeth, just before transfers from motor cycles was stopped.

Mervyn J. Fine.

1275 MG – Fortunately, reverse MG registrations aren't particularly rare. Consequently many can be found transferred to MG cars. This one, 1275 MG belongs to Robert Anderson of London.

1700 MG – Mrs. M. Greasby, Barbican, London EC2.

MH 4 – Michael Harrison of Appleby, Cumbria.

64 MMG – Ralph Villis, Paignton, Devon. He is

determind to resist offers that would split the original number from the original car.

MNJ 5 – Martyn Nigel Jones, a motor trader from Swansea.

1 MOG – For the uninitiated, a MOG, is the enthusiast's term for a Morgan car. Grahame N. Bryant of Woburn, who owns MOG 1 as well as 1 MOG, must surely be the envy of all Morgan owners.

41 MOK – or "For I'm O.K.". The property of

Tony Cutter, a Police Officer with the Wiltshire Constabulary. For obvious reasons, he has resisted the temptation to space out the number.

9981 MP – Mark Fairman of Trowbridge. Spaced to read 998 IMP on the 1969 Sunbeam Imp Sport.

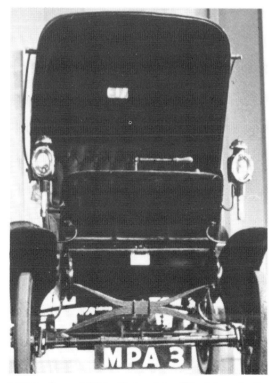

MPA 3 – 1901 Columbia Electric at the National Motor Museum, Beaulieu.

MRL 1P – (Mr. Lip) Michael Priestman of London.

MTP 1 – A classic registration mark on a classic Volvo 1800 ES. The property of Mr. & Mrs. Walker from Christchurch, Dorset.

MUM 1 – Owned by number one Mum, Mrs M. Jackson of Cardiff. She attends most numbers rallies and has won a few prizes. The number was purchased by her husband as a present over twenty five years ago.

The number was originally on the Leeds Mayoral car. It became available when the plate was replaced with U 1.   Also in the family, HJ 3333.

97 MW, 800 MW and 6000 MW – Numbers enthusiast, Martin Williams from Swindon, has been a long time campaigner for the return of stolen registration marks. Some years ago, he had the misfortune of having XMW 11 stolen. Although the restriction on return of stolen marks is a hefty five years, at least it is a step in the right direction. Martin's collection is: 26 MW, 97 MW, 400 MW, 800 MW, 1947 MW (year of birth), and 6000 MW.

1500 N – Nigel Ferguson of Highcliffe, Dorset. Owned since 1980.

NCX 2 – Ford Escort 1.3L, driven by Mrs. Susan Johnson of Hull.

76 NEV and 96 NEV – Tony Nevett of Lymington, Hampshire, has owned the pair for several years.

NEW 303 – This number is on my new Granada Ghia. I did own the registration number MAY 342. However, I lost this like so many others at the time, due to the change of rules by the Licensing Authorities, being unable to put it on to retention while I brought a new vehicle. MAY 342 was the perfect number as my birth date is May 3rd '42. Mr. W. A. Wren, Billericay, Essex.

NGS 18 – Television has given the private detective an image of all action crime fighting. There's Canon, who has bullets whistling past his ears every ten minutes and Rockford who never gets the routine, small debt collection work. Their crime busting, makes them a target for many a crook.

Perhaps the last thing a private detective would seem to want, is a distinctive car registration number, let alone a number plate with his own initials. Peter Heims, a private detective from Leatherhead has been featured in this book with his distinctive number plate 00 2. Another private eye has declared his "not so private" image. He is Norman G. Sharp, from Newcastle-upon-Tyne, proprietor of "North East Enquiries and Trade Services Ltd.", a member of the Association of British Detectives. The number plate on his Ford Capri, is NGS 18. Although he would dearly love to own NGS 1, the "18" is the best alternative, as it is his lucky number.

Norman started his business at the age of 18, his office suite number is 18, he had a fair win on the football pools with a perm from 18, he plays 18 holes at golf and has an 18 handicap.

NKH 999 – Sam Schultz, director of Arncliffes of Hull. Motor traders and main area dealer for Lada cars. However, this number is on Mr. Schultz's Mercedes 230 E Saloon.

56 NPC – Mr. P. A. Corbridge, Ferryhill, Co. Durham. The number was purchased from a dealer in January 1983 and transferred to the Porsche 911.

1 NUR – There are several ways of reading this number plate. In you are. Inure. One only. The latter, being the German translation. It is owned by Michael Gerson of London, who also has in his collection, NUR 1, GER5ON, MJG 1, MJG 5, VAT 10, TAT 4, 05, ETA 1, 1 ETA, 6 JG, AG 131, SG 43 and 2000 PG.

O 110 – This attractive number is owned by Mr. F. Tandy, who is in the record business.

OD 1 – Peter Jones, Bristol. On a customised Mini. Also in the family; POD 1, POD 2, POD 3, POD 4, OD 3 and 1 DEB.

ODD 77 Mrs. J. H. Beavis of Lymington, Hampshire.

OHT 1M – (Oh Tim!) Tim Morris of Weston-Super-Mare, Avon.

OK 1 – The property of Charles Yeates from Loughborough, Leicestershire

ONE 7 – Mrs. O. Hacking, of Virginia Water, Surrey. 17 is her lucky number. The registration has remained in the family for many years. Husband owns BV 7.

ONY 1 – Tony Williams of Loudwater, Hertfordshire. He is a powerboat, world record holder.

002 – Peter Heims, a Leatherhead Private Investigator, always had aspirations to be a James Bond, but unfortunately fell 5 degrees below the required standard.

He does not mind, however, for although 007 is licensed to kill, 002 is licensed to love.

OO 5005 and SOO 500 – Cleverly spaced and styled to look like 500 500 and 005 005, by Mr. Ambridge of Colchester, Essex.

000 111 – Part of a collection of "000" registrations, owned by Harris Motors of Bristol.

OPA 4L – (OPAL well almost!) – White Horse Garage, Calne, Wiltshire.

OWN 1 – On a demonstrator car, owned by Coombs of Guildford.

1 OYA (LOYA) Morris Loya of Twickenham, Middlesex. This priceless gem (for Morris), was acquired in January 1982, complete with Alfa Romeo GTV 6.

PAR 15H (Parish) – Mrs. Inge Parish of London, has owned the number since 1970 and has no intention of ever letting it go out of the family.

PCS 3 – P. Carthew of Rickmansworth, Herts. On a Lotus Elan, Series III.

PDM 1L Paul D. Milsom of Peterborough.

PDR 1 – Mr. & Mrs. Rowe of Stapleford, Nottingham.

PEP 51 (PEPSI) – This plate was owned for many years by John Keen, who traded as Pepsi Car Numbers. After he sold the registration, he changed his trading name to Autoplates. He sold the number to Martin Taplin of Chesham, Buckinghamshire.

3342 PG – Cheddar Valley Coaches have taken advantage of the latest transfer rules and have had the number 3342 PG transferred to one of their coaches. The vehicle is subject to PSV testing and until 10th January, 1983, did not qualify as a recipient vehicle for cherished transfer.

1 PH – Mr. P. Hopkins of London. This valuable number is currently on a Jaguar XJS.

PHR 1 and PHR 7. – Mr. P. H. Reid of Harrow, Middlesex.

PLE 999 – Owned by Mr. G. J. D. Bruce and housed at Beaulieu, Museum.

PLS 1 – Paul Lester Silburn of Broughton, Kettering, Northamptonshire. Also owns PS 1111.

PNA 11 – Don and Anne Nisbet, PNA Ltd, Wimborne.

29 PNM – The number came into my possession

on the 2nd April 1982. The number was originally on a Morris 6cwt van, which had been registered on 18.8.64.

I bought the van for £250 through a newspaper advertisement and the vendor drove it down to London from Balsock for me. The man told me that the chassis number on the log book was wrong, but not to worry. The number on the log book said MAU 5175978 and on the van it was "V". The man said just alter it on the log book and it will be O.K. This I did. When the log book came back from D.V.L.C. Swansea, the chassis number had not been altered, but the engine number had the corrected chassis number.

I took my cherished transfer application to Ruislip Licensing Office and explained what had happened. They told me that the transfer would fail. The chassis number had to be absolutely correct. I was very disappointed, as you can probably imagine.

The next day I went to the Licensing Office and asked to see the Manager, who was very helpful. He inspected the vehicle, there and then, stamped the log book and sent it off. When the document came back to me again, the chassis number was correct, to my relief. Later, the transfer of 29 PNM from the van to my Cortina, was completed.

I use the Cortina as a Mini-cab for Academy Cars, Hayes End, Middlesex, and they have given me a call sign of 29.

P. N. Marten, Hayes, Middlesex.

Note: If you buy a vehicle with a registration number, always check the chassis number before you part with any cash. An incorrect number can lose you the registration. When buying a number plate for the first time, it is advisable to use the services of a C.N.D.A. member. This should ensure a smooth transfer with a guarantee.

50 PP and 50 PPP – Paul P. Paterson, Sunderland. An attractive pair of registrations that were obtained with a considerable degree of luck. Also in the family, PEP 10.

PPP 6 – Trevor Nicosia, Aylesbury, Buckinghamshire.

PS 606 – Ronald Gair, Lerwick, Scotland.

37 PT – Steve Wood, Redcar, Cleveland.

PAU 1 (PAUL) – Paul Davis of Wandsworth, London, claims that he is the son of car number crazy parents. The family collection includes 5 D (SD) for father, Sid Davis, SYD 50, and the classic DAV 15 (DAVIS). Paul's brother Neville has 765 NEV on a Fiat X 19.

SHU 1 – Geoffrey Adler, Managing Director of Shu One Ltd., Footwear Distributors of North West London. The number was acquired and the Company named after the number plate.

37 PT – Steve Wood, Redcar, Cleveland. Renowned autonumerologist, having been interested in spotting car numbers for over fifteen years. Has supplied some of the photographs that appear in this book. As SW was proving rather difficult to find, Steve settled for the distinctive 37 PT and so realised his ambition to own a "special plate" himself.

Steve admits to being totally hooked on spotting car registrations. He cannot go on ANY journey without making a written record of all the interesting plates that he spots. On the day of the rally at Beaulieu (31st July 1983) he filled an entire notebook and claimed that he may be purchasing a dictaphone, for instant logging.

R 8 – Rob Walker of Frome, Somerset.

2400 PW – This photograph was taken by the owner, Paul Whyatt. He can be contacted for other number plate pictures, at Team Photographs, PO Box 137, Welwyn Garden City, Hertfordshire.

1000 R – Roger Preston, R & P Fashions, Leyburn, North Yorkshire.

77 PZ – Perry Zellick, Windsor, Berkshire. Owned since 1977 and now on a Plymouth Barracuda.

Commanding Officer, Group Captain Ken Lovett, with Flight Lieutenant Brian Otridge, in front of the two vehicles on the day of transfer.

13 RAF – Before disbanding in December 1981, Number 13 Squadron based at RAF Wyton, was presented with a Hillman Super Minx Estate Car bearing the registration '13 RAF'. After the squadron's disbandment, the Wyton Mechanical Transport Officer, Flight Lieutenant Brian Otridge, was tasked with perpetuating the cherished number until the squadron reforms in 1987.

It became evident that the 1963 vehicle bearing the registration would have rotted away by 1987, and as Department of Transport Regulations demanded that the donor vehicle in a transfer be taxed, plans were formulated to transfer the number at an early stage. The RAF Wyton welfare bus, a 1981 Leyland Sherpa was selected as the best vehicle to carry the number forward to 1987 and on Tuesday 21 December 1982 the transfer was effected.

RAY 66 G – looking as legally as I can for 666, I am a RNC member and a Sheffield Club member, significance with 666 is the 3 sixes in Phone No. Birthday 16th, but I acquired the number for the RAY. Obviously I have been a mad autonumerologist for about 6 years. I would love to own RAY 10K (RAY 1 OK). My little boy Ben 2½ years is starting young as you can see, with his Tee shirt, (BEN 1 NOW 2) and number plate on his Jeep.

Anyone in the Sheffield area wanting to join the Sheffield RNC, please call in at the Florists where I work, House of Flowers, Ecclesall Road, and pick up a form.

Ray Drury
Sheffield

RDV 600 – Shaw Wedding Cars, Shaw, Melksham.

3890 RF – John Harrison, Newcastle-upon-

Tyne. A dedicated numbers enthusiast. Member of the R.N.C., and Europlate, (an international club for those interested in spotting different types of number plate from other countries). Personally, I cannot see the fascination, as the U.K., cherished numbers game is so much more interesting than the non-transferrable and largely unattractive plates from other countries. However, John is an authority on U.K., issues as well as an international plate expert. He can talk to you for hours about the various issues that have come from Licensing Authorities over the years.

1500 RO – Bill Ferguson, of Highcliffe, Dorset.

RGU 1 – Roger Glen Urquart of Kenley, Surrey.

ROB 2 – Rob Walker, Garage Proprietor, Frome, Somerset.

ROD 814, BOB 964 and JON 304 – It is not unheard of for directors of a company to have distinctive registration numbers. However, it is unusual for all the directors to have their first names on number plates.

Rodney Fraser, Robert Snaith and John Lovegrove are the directors of English Rose (Motor Body Repairs) Ltd. of Gosport. Hampshire. Their registration numbers are ROD 814. BOB 964 and JON 304.

RJT 1 – Mr. R. J. Tanner of Bristol. Owned since 1970 and transferred several times since.

RR 1 – Possibly the most valuable car registration number in the world, with a value in the region of £25,000. Owned by H.R. Owen Ltd. of London, (Rolls-Royce distributors).

RO 115, 181 D and 11 COB – David & Maggie Brown of Purley, Surrey. This superb collection of numbers enhance the family collection of cars. RO 115 looking remarkably like "ROLLS" on the Rolls-Royce Corniche Convertible. 181 D looking like 1 BID (incidentally, David missed 501 D (SOLD) by a matter of hours), on a 320 BMW. 11 COB on the 427 AC Cobra.

This unique set gives them great fun, when all the cars are together. They also claim that it has brought them extra business.

RU 18 – One of the classic "fun numbers". It has changed hands at least four times in the last ten years. Although the number plate can be seen in many public houses, these are worthless plates used as a gimmick to deter under age drinking.

The rightful owner is John Steele of Leeds. It is on an E Type Jaguar. RU 18 was the overall winner of the 1982 R.N.C. Numbers Rally at Harewood House.

48 RW – Robert Williams, Motherwell, Lanarkshire, Scotland. A winner at the 1982 Registration Numbers Club Rally.

S 27 – Lord Strathcarron of Beaulieu, Hampshire. The number is on a 1903 Georges Richard Brougham and is on display at the nearby National Motor Museum.

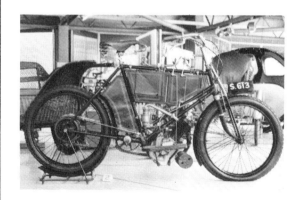

S 613 – National Motor Museum, Beaulieu. On a 1904 Phaensi Motorcycle.

SAM 388 – Sam Ellis from Lurgan, County Armagh, Northern Ireland. A dedicated car numbers enthusiast, who attends many Car Numbers Rallies, and could hold a record for total distance travelled to Rallies.

SA 72 – Owned by Mr. B. Richardson of Middlesex. Displayed on the original 1903 Peugeot.

SAM 323 – Samuel Alan Murray of Inverurie, Scotland. On a Volvo 343 DL.

SAN 2 – San Duncan of Glasgow. The car was hand built from scratch. The number plate adds the finishing touch.

SCG 234 – Steve and Carol Gibbs of Tipton, West Midlands. Supporters of many rallies and winners at the 1982 Registration Numbers Club event.

SEW 1 – Ray Rushton, The Wimbledon Sewing Machine Company, London. He also owns SEW 1 N (Sewing).

STT 1 & 4000 DT – Part of the Teddy Turner family collection. Teddy owns TT 100 and 55 TTT. STT 1 = Sallie Ann Turner, 4 HTT for Harold Teddy Turner & 1956 DT on David Turner's 1956 Ford Thunderbird.

SCT 10 – Stephen C. Templeton of Swansea. Photographed here with his wife, Denise. Member of the Registration Numbers Club.

SDJ 1 – Terrence Lennon from St. Helens, Merseyside. The number is originally from St. Helens.

SEP 19 – John Morris, Birmingham. Owned for six years.

SGN 2 – Mr. H. Edginton of Newton Ferrers. On a 1971 280 SE Mercedes.

SH 100 – Mr. & Mrs. S. Holtby of Beverley, North Humberside.

SJF 6 – Stephen John Frampton of Portsmouth. Cherished number dealer and member of the C.N.D.A.

SM 21 – Dr. J. Stewart Moffat of Carlisle, Cumbria. On a Ford Granada.

SN 2 – Eric Geddes of Dunblane, Perthshire.

SUM 1 – Mr. J. Wardell of Cottingham, Yorkshire, is the "someone" who owns this fun number.

SWL 9 and 9 SWL – It had always been my great ambition to own a personalised number plate and I was lucky enough to acquire 9 SWL through an advertisement in 1976 just prior to the DVLC dispute.

Two years later when returning from a long journey, only 5 miles from home, I spotted my twin approaching in the opposite direction – another Mini with the reverse number plate – SWL 9. I just couldn't believe it and after completing a speedy U-turn and giving chase found SWL 9 had pulled into a garage, (the doors just starting to close) as the hydrolastic suspension had collapsed! The owner, a policeman, said he would be only too pleased to sell! and hey presto!, a very lucky deal was struck.

I soon arranged for the suspension to be repaired and have only just parted with the car after miles of happy motoring and my great ambition has been two fold.

Stephen Latimer, Wells

SYB 1L – Sybil Howgego of Hatfield, Hertfordshire. Has won several prizes at number rallies.

87

TBW 6, TBW 90 and TBW 152 – Terry Bracey Wright owns this set for business and pleasure purposes. Vehicles used in his Automobile Engineering business at Wingrave, Aylesbury, Buckinghamshire, are clearly enhanced with the personalised numbers.

URA 2 (You are a two) – Mr. B. A. Middleton's 1956 Rolls-Royce Silver Cloud I. A great number for his firm Bridal Services Ltd., of 170 Selsdon Road, South Croydon, Surrey. The car is used for weddings, for which the number is particularly appropriate.

T 25 – Owned by the Intercom Shipping Agency of London.

1 TAR – The perfect plate for "Driveways", Asphalt and Tarmacadam Contractors, of Canford Cliffs, near Bournemouth.

5 TAR (STAR) – Robin Colville of Calverley, Leeds, has this classic registration number on his 1977 Jaguar XJS.

TAX 1 (TAXI) – One morning in 1959 when I was a totally uncontrollable car cleaner and general dogsbody, a man arrived at Welbeck Motors, the famous London mini cab firm, with a terribly tired and rusty old Vanguard and announced that he intended to sell my boss, Michael Gotla, his car for £200. When the laughter had died down in the showroom, the man insisted that we looked more carefully at his car, and then to our amazement we found it bore the number TAX1.

After a great deal of haggling, cries of distress and arms in the air, a compromise was reached of £75 in cash, a ploughmans lunch in the local pub, and a return 3rd class fare to Cardiff. The number plate was immediately transferred to a red Renault Dauphine and became London's first Welbeck Mini Cab. (The Vanguard was also sold for £40). Soon after, I became a director of the firm.

A year later in a weak moment, probably when ski slopes were calling and I had no money, I sold it to a Taxi firm in Basingstoke with a new fleet of Ford Cortinas. This company got into financial difficulties, and some six months later I had to repossess the entire fleet – and to my delight TAX1 was among them. Shortly after this, Welbeck Motors ceased trading, and I became a Director of Walton Lodge Garage (where I still clean the loos and make the tea!!! 'cause nobody else will)!

The number plate has been on at least 18 different vehicles since then including Range

Rovers, Fords, Audis, and V.W.'s. It is currently on a new 1800 cc VW Golf GTi, and enjoys low level flying from Thames Ditton to Walton every day.

One of the more memorable moments happened a couple of years ago, when TAXI was on a new Range Rover and a party of friends went skiing to Verbier. Whether it was the eleven people hanging all over the vehicle or they thought I was plying for hire, I never really did find out, but the Swiss police decided to take an extremely serious view of the situation, and we were all arrested and put in a cell while they checked, through their computer in Geneva, whether the number plate was true or false.

I was eventually released after an "interview" for three hours. "Vee do not allow zees stupid number plates in zis country", I was told by a thick-set, totally humourless, part-time policeman.

Most officials in Europe recognise that the English are a little eccentric, and accept that cherished numbers create a little amusement in these days of bureaucracy, red tape, and mundane motor cars.

Hugh Ruding-Bryan, Walton-on-Thames, Surrey

late Austin A35 has covered over 132,000 miles and still has the original engine.

4 TEA – The number plate and vehicle are the pride and joy of Mr. Wilson from Haworth, Yorkshire. He is a director of Yorkshire Biscuits Ltd., and he also owns the number plate 4000 TW.

TAY 2 – Mr. R. Taylour of Rugby, Warwickshire. Award winner at the Longleat Rally, August 1982. Also in the family, TAY 200

TBK 1 – Mr. & Mrs. H. Coward of Portsmouth. Class 3 winner at Longleat 1982. The immacu-

TEN 66 – Mr. Morphy of Bury photographed here as he collects his prize at the 1979 R.N.C. Rally from the Deputy Lord Mayor of Leeds, Councillor Ron Challenor.

THE 7 – In more ways than one, Cyril May of Canterbury, has "THE 7". It is on an immaculate Austin Seven.

TJ 1 – This valuable and rare registration, is owned by Jim Jackson of Cleveland. His wife drives TJ 10.

TME 666 – Robert Onions of Loughborough, Leicestershire. On a 1948 Morris Eight.

TOP 10 – Not the property of a chart topping popstar, but Edwin Marriott, a builder from Chesterfield.

TR 4 – Owned by Mr. G. Williams of Pinner. When holidaying in Germany, Mr. Williams met the owner of SR TR 4, by sheer chance ... It transpired that SR are the letters denoting Straubing and the owner had actually moved address temporarily, just to acquire this number when it was due for allocation.

I U – At first glance, you may think that this size of number plate (see photograph), is illegal. However, it is not. The plate complies with the regulations. It is owned by John Hudson of Stafford.

16 UHU – Peter Cripps of Kidlington, Oxfordshire was in a sticky situation when he couldn't obtain his initials and eventually settled for 16 UHU.

6 UNN – BMW 528 pictured here at the 1977 Rally at Dodington. The car and number is owned by John Gunn of Dunfermline.

USA 3 – Quentin Henderson of Blairgowrie, Perthshire, is lucky to still be the owner. He left it in the care of Rev. Ainslie Walton of Torbrex whilst he travelled round the world. After six years abroad, Quentin returned to hear all the stories of the changes of transfer rules and how the Rev. Walton managed to retain the number. The photograph shows Miss Pamela Walton, keeping a guarding hand on the car.

VBT 1 – When owner, Mr. H. Speck of Driffield, found his home town moved from Yorkshire to North Humberside, in boundary changes, his car registration number VBT 1, took on a new significance. The registration was first issued in 1958 by the East Riding of Yorkshire, Local Authority. Mr. Speck is proud to own one of Yorkshire's number one number plates.

863 VC – Valerie Cox of Sunningdale, Berkshire, has the number on a Mercedes.

VCL 1 – Victor C. Lukaniuk, Brandon, Suffolk.

VN 1000 – L. Thackray of Old Malton, North Yorkshire. Originally allocated on 1st January 1930, to a BSA Motorcycle, (total cost £36). Mr. Thackray bought the bike and number in 1966 for £15 and now claims that his car is one of very few to sport a number plate with 1000.

VRW 1 – The perfect registration mark for Victor Raymond Waters, of Stafford. The plate complements the fine example Bentley.

VTG 1 – Geoffrey Grundy of Barnsley, South Yorkshire.

1300 VW – On a 1300 VW, owned by Volkswagen distributors, Weir Lodge, Chertsey, Surrey.

546 WF – Mr. W. Foley, Flixton, Manchester.

WET 7 – Keith Gould's Amphicar. The car was the 1964 Earls Court Motor Show Car. It was purchased by Keith in 1975 and the number was bought in 1976.

1 WHU – Rodney Cuff, Frome, Somerset. Proprietor of a garage business. The number is on a Volkswagen Motorhome.

WJD 1. – My family's Company is W.J. Daniel & Co. Ltd. Whilst I drive the Mercedes pictured above, my brother has WJD 3. Michael Daniel, Windsor, Berkshire.

WJJ 2 – W. J. Joyce of Trowbridge, Wiltshire. Engineer and Land Rover specialist.

WMX 1 – George Graves, Brigg, South Humberside. Displayed on a limited edition Volvo 262 C, two door Coupe.

WNA 1 – William Nicholls Associates, Yam, Cleveland. They also own WNA 2.

WS 333 – Walter Stern, St. John's Wood, London.

WT 1 – This early Yorkshire registration number, has remained in the county of origin, thanks to owner Roger Waterfall of Skipton.

X 825 – 1906 Renault, part of the Montagu collection at Beaulieu.

XJ5 (XJS) – On a Jaguar XJS owned by Maurice Worton of Kidderminster, Worcestershire.

XVX 111 – B. Clark, Loughton, Essex. Was transferred for the seventh time since 1954, to the present Fiat 130 coupe.

YFC 1 – In 1942, the three gentlemen pictured above, decided to form a Young Farmers Club in the St. Neots area. The trio, all aged 21, formed a

committee. Harry was chairman and Rex was secretary, John was also on the committee.

A few years later, John emigrated to Kenya and nine years ago he set up home in Australia. He is now proprieter of a contracting business in Perth. He returned to England on a holiday and was delighted to find that the St. Neots Young Farmers Club was thriving. His nephew, Andrew Willmer has acquired the registration mark YFC 1 and has become the envy of St. Neots Young Farmers Club.

The number plate makes a superb setting for a re-union photograph of the founding trio. Left to right: John Willmer, Harry Chapman and Rex Aubrey.

YHH 99 York House Hotel, Eastbourne, Sussex.

YL 9 – 1922 Phanomobil. A three wheeler van, made in Germany. On display at the National Motor Museum.

Junior Section

Many children are fascinated by car numbers and spotting them has been a hobby for decades. In 1980 the JUNIOR NUMBER SPOTTERS CLUB was founded as a feature of Car Numbers Monthly.

Membership is FREE to any person aged up to 16, by sending a stamped addressed envelope to Car Numbers Monthly, (Junior Section), P.O. Box 1, Bradford-on-Avon, Wiltshire, BA15 1YQ. A newsletter will be forwarded.

At the end of each year, the most dedicated Junior Number Spotter is awarded the title of Junior Number Plate Spotter of the year. The 1980 award, went to Adrian Bartlett, pictured below, being presented with the trophy by T.V. personality Shaw Taylor.

Adrian was also treated to a guided tour of the I.T.N., Studios in London. He was also interviewed on BBC Radio 1 and HTV

The most important rule of club membership, is road safety. Junior Number Spotters are not recommended to note every number plate that goes by. It is the distinctive registrations, such as those listed in this book, that are of prime interest.

It is always a thrill to see a distinctive registration on a car, especially when you have spotted it for the first time. Keep in mind, that the owner has probably spent a lot of money, time and effort in retaining it. You will please the owner, by showing an interest in his registration number, after all, he probably bought it to proudly display it.

Please note that the Junior Number Spotters Club, is not connected with the Registration Numbers Club.

Many games can also be played, involving car number plates, whilst travelling in the car. Why not try some of the following games:-

Score points for number plates that spell words or names. Score 5 points for spotting a number plate with three consecutive letters spelling a word or name. Example: ROD, THE, ANN. Score 10 points for spotting a registration with just two or three consecutive letters that spell a word. Example: AT, AN, ON. Score 10 points for spotting a registration with two or three consecutive letters that denote an abbreviation (as listed in the Oxford Dictionary). Example: GB, USA, MP, JP, DR. Score 20 points for spotting a number plate relevant to the vehicle. Example: 397 BMW on a BMW car. 8261 MG on an MG car.

Andrew & Tracey Crisp of Knowle, Solihull.

Andrew and Tracey are keen members of the Junior Numbers Spotters Club. They are pictured, with their mother's number, JCR 15P, cleverly spaced by Mrs. Joan Crisp to read, J. CRISP. The number won first prize at the Beaulieu Numbers Rally in 1976.

Why not try the "Mathematics game", using the digits on number plates?

Depending on your age and the standard you have reached, you could choose one of the following games:-

Start with a single number 1, that you have spotted, (example XYA 1 R or 1 EAT etc.....) and then look for single "2" and then "3" and so on.

Start by looking for three consecutive numbers, (i.e. 123) and then look for 234 and then 345 and so on.

If you are good at mental arithmetic, then look for number plates with corresponding numbers to the letter in the alphabet. For example, look for ABC 123, A = last letter and so on.

Few parents will admit to naming their children after personalised number plates already held in the family, however, it is known that it does happen. It saves a lot of hassle trying to find a suitable registration if a registration number is bought before the child is born and afterwards, name the child to suit the registration.

The Grant family of Trowbridge, already had 26 PG and when their son was born, they may claim that it was pure coincidence that they named him Peter.

The Tyndales went one better, Jill and Adrian have named both of their children with the same initials. The cherished number is 8000 AT and the children are Amelia and Andrew.

Is it yet another coincidence that Stephen John Howse of Gerrads Cross has named his son Stephen James Howse and the car registration is 6 SJH,?

The C.N.D.A. & R.N.C.

C.N.D.A. are the designatory letters used by the members of the Cherished Numbers Dealers Association Limited. The majority of companies dealing with cherished numbers are members of the Association, and all are bound to trade in a manner acceptable to the C.N.D.A., Articles of Association, thereby giving would-be purchasers of cherished numbers certain assurances.

The first meeting of cherished numbers dealers, which ultimately led to the formation of C.N.D.A., was at the Motor Show in 1971. Whilst several individuals had been dealing in cherished numbers for some little time, the appearance of additional advertisers made personal contact desirable. It was decided that a further meeting should take place, to which all dealers should be invited.

In the 'early days', some ten years ago, the sales of registration numbers flourished as there was very little restriction on their transfer. At the meeting, which took place in the Midlands, most of the established dealers attended which gave an opportunity for everyone present to put faces to names. Naturally there were differences of opinion, but these were resolved and it was proposed that an organisation be formed. So P.N.D.A. (Personalised Numbers Dealers Association) came into being with a code of practise for its members and some degree of assurance for their clients. Annual cherished numbers rallies were organised by P.N.D.A. at several venues, and were well attended and supported.

By 1976 the computerisation of vehicle records was well under way, utilising the central system at Swansea and a combination of the old local taxation offices, and the new vehicle licensing offices. The transfer of cherished numbers was 'tightened up' with requirements introduced which made transfer of just the number from a registration book very difficult, if not impossible. P.N.D.A. was now firmly established and having made representation to the Swansea licensing centre had become officially recognised. As a result it was decided to change the name of the association to Cherished Numbers Dealers Association Limited, in keeping with the Department of Transport terminology for personalised numbers.

The Cherished Numbers Dealers Association Limited is primarily a trade association which in addditon to representing the interests of its membership and cherished number owners officially to the Department of Transport, also offers the public an assurance in respect of its member companies.

The address of the Cherished Numbers Dealers Association is: The Secretary, 10/12 Cornard Road, Sudbury, Suffolk, CO10 6XA.

The Registration Numbers Club was founded in 1976 by Alex Jackson, of Scarcroft Leeds. (He owns 1 AGJ, 2 AGJ, 8 AGJ, AJ 3, AYJ 1, YEL 4).

The aims of the club are to help members with transfer difficulties and to ensure smooth running of the transfer system. It is a non-profit making organisation, although various items are sold, to boost club funds. Amongst these, is a hand engraved enamelled badge, that will elegantly complement the most prestigious badge bar. You can have your own registration number engraved on the badge.

The annual R.N.C. Rally is the highlight of the year. Always well organised and well attended. The 1980 venue was Newby Hall, near Ripon and 1981 was Nostell Priory, near Wakefield.

Anyone is welcome to join the club, whether or not they own a distinctive registration. The membership is now in the region of 3,000 and rising weekly. If you would like to join, write to :- The Secretary, Registration Numbers Club, 81 Station Parade, Harrogate, Yorkshire.

Diplomatic Vehicles

Ambassadors and High Commissioners have specially allocated numbers for vehicles used in Great Britain.

Although it is not always easy to identify these marks, known as CD plates (Corps Diplomatique), they can be identified when the give away CD does not appear on the vehicle, by the special tax disc on the windscreen.

Some desirable registration numbers have been issued to CD vehicles, such as in the photographs shown here. They are allocated by DVLC, Swansea as a special concession and are transferrable from one car to another, provided that is to the same owner.

A DVLC spokesman confirmed that it would not be possible to sell any of these special marks.

THE following list, is of distinctive numbers used on diplomatic vehicles in Great Britain. Many of these numbers can be spotted in London.

1 AFG	– Afghanistan
1 ARG	– Argentina
AUS 1	– Australia
1 OES	– Austria
BHA 1B	– Bahamas
BAH 1	– Bahrein
BDH 1	– Bangladesh
BDS 1	– Barbados
1 BE	– Belgium
DAH 1	– Benin Rep.
BOT 1	– Botswana
BRZ 1	– Brazil
BG 1	– Bulgaria
BUR 1	– Burma
1 CAM	– Cameroon
CAN 1	– Canada
QUE 1	– Quebec
1 CHI	– Chile
CHN 1	– China
COL 1	– Columbia
1 CZE	– Czechoslovacia
1 DAN	– Denmark
DOM 300	– Dominican R.
1 ECU	– Ecuador

ELS 1	– El Salvador
ETH 325R	– Ethiopia
FIJ 1	– Fiji
FRA 1	– France
1 GAB	– Gabon
1 GER	– German F.R.
1 GHA	– Ghana
GRE 1 S	– Greece
1 GRN	– Grenada
GYA 1	– Guyana
HAI 1	– Haiti
HON 2	– Honduras
HXG 1C	– Hong Kong

1 CEM	– Iceland
IND 1	– India
RI 1	– Indonesia
1 PER	– Iran

ISR 1	– Israel
ITA 1	– Italy
1 RCI	– Ivory Coast
1 JAM	– Jamaica
JPB 1D	– Japan
HKJ 111	– Jordan
1 KEN	– Kenya
1 KOR	– Korea, Rep.
1 KUW	– Kuwait
RL 1	– Lebanon
1 LES	– Lesotho
LIB 1	– Liberia
1 LUX	– Luxembourg
1 MLW	– Malawi
1 M	– Malaysia
1 MLT	– Malta
MAU 1	– Mauritius
NEP 1	– Nepal
NL 1	– Netherlands
NZ 1	– New Zealand
NIC 1	– Nicaragua

FGN 1	– Nigeria
1 NWY	– Norway
OMA 1N	– Oman
PAK 1	– Pakistan
PAN 1	– Panama
1 PNG	– Papua New Guinea
PE 1	– Peru
PHI 1	– Philippines
1 POR	– Portugal

QTR 1	– Qatar

1 ROM	– Romania
SAO 1L	– Saudi Arabia

SEN 1	– Senegal
SEY 1	– Seychelles
HSL 1	– Sierra Leone
SGP 1	– Singapore
SA 1	– South Africa
SPA 1N	– Spain
CEY 1	– Sri Lanka
SUD 1	– Sudan
1 SZL	– Swaziland
SVE 1	– Sweden
TAN 1	– Tanzania
THA 12	– Thailand
1 TON	– Tonga

1 TT	– Trinidad & Tobago
TUN 1	– Tunisia
1 TUR	– Turkey
1 UGA	– Uganda
USA 1	– U.S.A.
1 SU	– U.S.S.R.
1 RUV	– Upper Volta
1 ROU	– Uruguay
1 VEN	– Venezuela
RYN 1	– Vietnam
YEM 1	– Yemen P.D.R.
ZAI 1	– Zaire
ZAM 1	– Zambia

United States System

When my research for this section of the book started, I struck a chord with personalised number plate buffs across the Atlantic. They just couldn't believe the complications and bureaucracy involved with the U.K., system. They were fascinated at the vast sums of money changing hands.

There is no red tape involved in acquiring a personal plate. The applicant simply applies to the State issuing office with his desired combination of letters and/or numbers. Provided it does not exceed six characters, the plate can read anything (within reason).

The system provides a vast choice. For example if SMITH is already taken, then you could try SMITH 1 to 9 and also in reverse. There can be fifty one identical plates in the States. However, on each plate is the name of the issuing State, which does make each one unique.

Personalised plates are known throughout the States as "Vanity Plates". Perhaps we are too vain in Great Britain to call our personalised plates "Vanity Plates", after all, if you refer to the dictionary you will find one definition, "ostentatious display", and ostentatious is defined as "pretentious display of wealth or luxury, showing off, attempt or intention to attract notice".

The USA system of personalised plates is so completely different. For a start, the number plates themselves couple as licenses and registration plates. There are some variations across the States, but Illinois, provides a typical example.

A personalised plate can be purchased from the State and can be allocated to a passenger car or motorcycle. The fee is a once only payment of $50 and $25 respectively. An additional fee of $10 is charged annually for the personalised plate, on top of the license renewal. In the U.K., tax discs have to be bought and displayed on the windscreen, to indicate that the licence has been paid for, and when it expires. In the U.S.A., a validity sticker is placed on the actual number plate, annually. There are also one year plates that are just renewed and discarded like an old validity sticker.

Discarded plates create great interest and are sold according to how rare the plate is. Value is added because each plate is made by the State. There is no such thing as the motorist making his own number plate, as in the U.K., plates are of no real value. In the States, there are magazines and believe it or not, conventions on the subject. Hundreds of people attend these conventions up to four times a year. The talk is all number plates and they last for anything up to four days, with an auction of the discarded plates on the final day. Such activity is as foreign to the U.K., scene as ours is to them.

An example of a Vermont plate as used by Paul Rawden of New Haven, is depicted below. The validity sticker is in the bottom right hand corner.

The U.S.A., system does not provide the facility for owners to sell their personalised plates. Furthermore, it is so easy and cheap to obtain such a plate, the glamour and status of ownership doesn't compare at all with the U.K., system.

A personalised plate can be lost if the owner moves his home to another State. If the combination was already being used by someone else in the new State, then an alternative would have to be chosen. However, some States permit the old plates to be used until the expiry date of the

PERSONALIZED LICENSE PLATE REQUEST FORM

VEHICLE OWNER'S
NAME _____

ADDRESS _____

CITY_____ STATE _____ ZIP _____

TELEPHONE   (HOME)_____( )_____ (WORK)_____( )_____
                        AC   AC

If motorcycle, ✔ here: ◯ Under 150 cc's
VEHICLE NO. 1   ◯ 150 cc's or over

Present License Plate No.
_____

If motorcycle, ✔ here: ◯ Under 150 cc's
VEHICLE NO.2   ◯ 150 cc's or over

Present License Plate No.
_____

1ST CHOICE	2ND CHOICE	3RD CHOICE

validity sticker and some insist on immediate change. Presumably for security reasons, the official cars used by the President and Vice-President, do not have distinctive registration numbers. They are standard issue.

Applications for personalised plates are dealt with on a first-come, first-served basis. They take approximately two months to be manufactured and sent by mail to the applicant. Above is a personalised plate request form, as used by Illinois. Again, far removed from the U.K., system.

Plates are also issued with categories of vehicle stamped on them in bold letters. Conditions must be met before a vehicle will qualify. For example; FERT SPREADER can only be used for a self-propelled, fertiliser-spreading vehicle operating within a 50 mile radius of the point from which it was loaded. It is also limited to a maximum speed of 30 mph. A registration number also appears on the plate .

When a car is sold, the personalised plate can be transferred to the owner's new car. The fee is approximately $10, (a fraction of the U.K. extortion – dosen't it make you sick?).

In California a veteran vehicle carries a **HORSELESS CARRIAGE** plate (see photograph below).

Irish Registrations

ANY registration number that has been allocated to a vehicle in Northern Ireland can be transferred, (subject to the usual conditions as described on the form V 317), in the U.K.

Registration numbers allocated in the Republic of Ireland cannot be transferred in the United Kingdom.

A couple of cases involving Irish registrations, spring to mind. Firstly, LIZ 1, which was registered to a vehicle by the County Mayo authorities in 1963. Some nineteen years later the number was registered to a vehicle in the United Kingdom, presumably the original 1963 car, via the DVLC computer and the owner was in possession of a V5 document. I remember him being quite upset when he learnt that it could not be transferred to another vehicle in the U.K. He even contacted the C.N.D.A., who double checked and confirmed that it was not transferrable. If DVLC did by chance accidentally permit a transfer of this mark at some stage, it is my opinion that they should transfer it again and again. However, the golden rule is to check with DVLC (in writing) whether or not a certain Irish number can be transferred, before buying or selling.

When either a number is to be transferred to or from a Northern Ireland vehicle, both the donor and recipient need to be registered on the same licensing system (i.e., either at DVLC or at a Northern Ireland Taxation Office). This can cause numerous problems and transfers can be delayed for anything up to a year.

Northern Ireland still use the old style green log book system of registering vehicles and records are maintained at Local Taxation Offices. A computerised vehicle record system is proposed to be introduced in Northern Ireland, in 1986.

From 30th November 1983, any U.K., mark issued in England, Scotland or Wales and currently registered at a Northern Ireland Taxation Office, will only be entitled to transfer throughout the U.K., if it was registered at some time at DVLC. This policy is due to the centralisation of records at Swansea, for example, if an English number was transferred and registered in London under the old Local Taxation Office system and was then shipped across to Northern Ireland, that number will not be transferrable in England, Scotland or Wales after 30th November 1983, unless the owner had made a written claim to DVLC for rights to the mark, prior to that date.

Two examples of Irish numbers; pictured above, IIA 111 issued by County Antrim (transferrable throughout the U.K.), and 147 FIK issued by County Dublin (not transferrable), pictured below.

From 1966 a new series of registrations were introduced in Northern Ireland to differentiate between other U.K. registrations. Three letters were followed by up to four numbers. The introduction of this series meant that year letters were not required.

If there were not so many difficulties in transfer, Northern Ireland numbers would sell like hot cakes, as cover numbers, to rid year letters as allocated on the mainland.

However, it is not popular any way to have such numbers and as the difficulties are not likely to be eased for the foreseeable future, the market is likely to remain dormant.

From 1904 to 1922 the United Kingdom was responsible for allocations to vehicles in Southern Ireland. When it became an Independent state in 1922, the original system of registering was maintained, hence the similarity. Number plates in Ireland can be white (front) and red (rear), with black letters and digits.

NORTHERN IRELAND ISSUES

AZ	Belfast	IZ	Armagh
BZ	Down	MZ	Belfast
CZ	Belfast	NZ	Londonderry
DZ	Antrim	OI	Belfast
EZ	Belfast	OZ	Belfast
FZ	Belfast	PZ	Belfast
GZ	Belfast	RZ	Antrim
HZ	Tyrone	SZ	Down
IA	Antrim	TZ	Belfast
IB	Armagh	UI	Londonderry
IJ	Down	UZ	Tyrone
IL	Fermanagh	WZ	Belfast
IW	Londonderry	XI	Belfast
JI	Tyrone	XZ	Armagh
JZ	Down	YZ	Londonderry
KZ	Antrim		

REPUBLIC OF IRELAND ISSUES

AI	Meath	PI	Cork C.B.
BI	Monaghan	RI	Dublin
CI	Laoighis	TI	Limerick
DI	Roscommon	WI	Waterford
EI	Sligo	YI	Dublin
FI	Tipperary North Riding	Z	Dublin
HI	Tipperary South Riding	ZA	Dublin
IC	Carlow	ZB	Cork
ID	Cavan	ZC	Dublin
IE	Clare	ZD	Dublin
IF	Cork	ZE	Dublin
IH	Donegal	ZF	Cork C.B.
IK	Dublin	ZH	Dublin
IM	Galway	ZJ	Dublin
IN	Kerry	ZK	Cork
IO	Kildare	ZL	Dublin
IP	Kilkenny	ZM	Galway
IR	Offaly	ZN	Neath
IT	Leitrim	ZO	Dublin
IU	Limerick	ZP	Donegal
IX	Longford	ZR	Wexford
IY	Louth	ZT	Cork
IZ	Mayo	ZU	Dublin
KI	Waterford	ZW	Kildare
LI	Westmeath	ZX	Kerry
MI	Wexford	ZY	Louth
NI	Wicklow		

Car Number Rallies

In recent years the CNDA haven't organised many rallies because of the immense amount of organisation required and quite frankly most dealers are too busy to get involved. The R.N.C., must be heartily congratulated on splendidly organised rallies. They make a special point of giving prizes to as many people as possible and they alternate awards, year by year to regular rally goers. The prizes are really just for fun, although one cannot help feeling that those entrants who don't receive anything, are really quite disappointed. It is noticeable that some of the unlucky ones depart with haste. Fortunately, most people treat it all as just a good day out. Even if you don't own a distinctive number yourself, you are sure to enjoy these intriguing gatherings.

Two Rolls-Royce cars at the 1981 Dodington Rally.

The 1981 Dodington rally was marred by the Showbiz Car Club. Some six months prior to the event, I had met officials of the Club, at their London office to discuss the possibilities of the proceeds from the rally, going to their organisation in return for several well known stars of television to attend the event. They were very keen and plans were set in motion. I was invited to several cocktail parties, that must have cost hundreds of pounds to put on. There were dozens of stars and the talk was all showbiz. They were certainly most enjoyable experiences. At each of these events I was promised big names for the rally and accordingly advertisements were placed in the national press to the effect that Stars would be there.

On the day of the rally it was a massive turnout, far more than the previous year, but not a single person turned up from the Showbiz Car Club. I was badly let down. There was no one to present the prizes, so a friend who is known as Jimmy Jimmy agreed to present them. Most people thought that with a name like Jimmy Jimmy he was a celebrity. He signed autographs and everyone was happy.

The only consolation was that the Showbiz Car Club did not receive a penny of the proceeds. This was donated to Dr.Barnardo's and they were designated as the charity to prosper from the 1982 rally at Longleat.

In recent years, Southport has become another rally venue, "No. 1" was spotted there.

THE first car numbers rally was held in 1973 and there has been at least one every year since then, at various venues throughout the country.

The rallies are of course, static. They are usually held in the grounds of stately homes.

The Cherished Numbers Dealers Association, originated the idea of rallies and in 1977, the Registration Numbers Club held their first annual rally.

Prizes, usually trophies, are awarded to the cars bearing the best registrations in their relevant classes.

Mr. M.A. Riley of Barnet, Herts, pictured here with his two entries in the 1977 CNDA Rally.

4851 PZ and 8674 JZ – Paul and John Zaringer of Bristol, joint owners of a Jewellery and Leather Goods business. The photograph was taken in August 1982 at the Longleat Car Numbers Rally.

Court Cases

There have been many cases of vehicles being sold with number plates that had already been transferred. One such case ended up in County Court in early 1982. The outline of the story was that a wealthy Lady instructed her Gardener to dispose of an old Humber car that had been stored on her Estate for six years. The Gardener had a look at the car and saw that it had a distinctive registration number. He then telephoned a dealer, claiming that this number was for sale with the car. The dealer then made an appointment with him to see the car and sent a representative one hundred miles. The dealer's representative assessed that approximately £400 would be needed to restore the vehicle to road worthy condition to obtain an M.O.T., pass in order that it could be licensed and then the number subsequently transferred. The dealer offered £30 for the car. The Gardener informed his employer of the offer and she accepted it. The dealer then spent £100 on having the vehicle collected via heavy goods vehicle transportation. However, when the car was being loaded on to the lorry, the Lady calmly told the dealer's representative, (who was present at the collection), that she wanted the old number plates from the car for sentimental reasons. It transpired that the number had been transferred six years previously, but the newly allocated registration number had not been fixed to the vehicle. The dealer was left with an old Humber that was surplus to requirements complete with a "C" registration mark, that had no market value. The dealer claimed £150 expenses from the lady, and she refused to pay.

In court, the dealer claimed that because the correct number plates for the vehicle, were not displayed, as prescribed under the Road Vehicles (Registration and Licensing) Regulations 1971, it constituted an offence under Section 22 of the Vehicles (Excise) Act 1971 and would render the person driving or keeping the vehicle, liable to prosecution under Section 28(4) of the Act. The Defendant should therefore be held responsible to pay the Plaintiff's out of pocket expenses for negligence.

The Defendant did not deny that the number plates were not as prescribed under the regulations. However, the Gardener who appeared as witness, denied that he had offered the registration number to the dealer.

The Registrar concluded that the number had been offered by the Gardener to the dealer, but as the Defendant did not intentionally sell the number, but only the old Humber car, the Plaintiff lost the case and was ordered to pay £20 costs.

The moral of the story is to check with the actual owner of the vehicle that the registration number is correct, rather than accept the word of a third party, no matter how well informed he may apear to be. The recommended course of action is to obtain a receipt from the owner, stating that the vehicle bearing the specific registration number has been sold at the agreed amount.

When the Department of Transport, London Enforcement Office, disputed various cherished transfer procedures with D.V.L.C., Swansea, several registration numbers were lost and considerable inconvenience was caused.

This dispute was the highlight of a County Court case. Basically, the plaintiff, (a number dealer), sought payment for a registration number transferred to his client's car. The Defendant, (the dealer's client) had refused to pay the money due, because the transfer had been delayed for a considerable period.

The case:- In August 1979, the defendant agreed to purchase a registration number for £270 and he forwarded his vehicle documents to the Plaintiff to enable the transfer application to be placed with the authorities. However, in a nutshell, one section of the Department of Transport approved the transfer system and another did not.

The D-O-T dispute continued for some seven months and the defendant asked for cancellation of the contract and the return of his documents. The Plaintiff agreed to cancel and promptly requested the return of all the papers from the Local Vehicle Licensing Office. However, the L.V.L.O., could not obtain the documents back from the London Enforcement Office. Meanwhile, the Defendant claimed that he had a buyer for his vehicle, a Rolls-Royce, and he desperately needed the documents. He blamed the Plaintiff for loss of sale of the car, because his intended purchaser would not buy the car without sight of the registration document. Furthermore, the Defendant counterclaimed the sum of £490, for lost use of the car, as it was illegal to drive a motor vehicle on the road without displaying a current excise licence.

The Plaintiff continually requested the return of the documents from the authorities and eventually the London Enforcement Office withdrew their involvement and the Local Vehicle Licensing Office were then in a position to complete the transfer, although, this was now October 1980. The Plaintiff produced documentary evidence that in October 1980 the Defendant again agreed to accept the registration number to be transferred to his car, provided it could be completed quickly. Indeed, the transfer was completed, only ten days later.

The Defendant refused to pay for the registration number after it had been transferred to his car. The Plaintiff sought the £270 due to him.

The Plaintiff produced written evidence from the Department of Transport stating:-

"Under Section 16 Road Vehicles (Registration and Licensing) Regulations 1971 it is an offence to fail to display a current Licence on a motor vehicle when kept or used on a public road. However, if the Licence is in the possession of the Licensing Authorities for amendment for whatever reason, although a fixed penalty ticket may be issued, the Ticket Office will normally waive any penalty on confirmation that a valid licence is in existence and that it is undergoing reissue.

The non-availability of a V5 registration document is no legal restriction on the disposal of a vehicle; the purchaser should be advised to complete a form V62 indicating that the previous owner has not been able to hand a V5 to him, and there is no fee payable in this instance.

The Plaintiff claimed that the D.O.T. statement proved that the vehicle could have been used on the road, whilst the application for transfer was pending, therefore the Defendant's counterclaim in respect of loss of use of the car, should be disregarded.

The Defendant also claimed that he had incurred various expenses in telephone calls and letters, furthermore, he had wasted a lot of time due to the inefficiency of the Plaintiff, to complete the transfer of the registration number in a reasonable period of time.

The Plaintiff stated that he had not been inefficent. He had placed the transfer application with his Local Vehicle Licensing Office, quickly and in good faith, It was this third party that were responsible for the excessive delay.

The case lasted three quarters of an hour, and neither party was represented by a solicitor.

Who do you think won the case? The important points of the case again; the Defendant had stated in writing in October 1980 that he still wished to have the number, despite all the prior problems. The delay incurred from the initial contract to completion was excessive and it is technically an offence to drive a vehicle on the road without displaying a tax disc. Could the defendant have applied for duplicate documents? The documents were not lost or stolen, they were known to be in existence and in safe hands, the Department of Transport. However, despite all the problems, in October 1980, the Defendant did agree, in writing, that he would still accept the registration number. The Defendant had not proved that the Plaintiff had been inefficient in his handling of the transfer, although the service provided by the third party, the Department of Transport, could not possibly be termed as efficient.

The result was that the Plaintiff won the case and awarded the £270 plus costs.

Size and Format of Number Plates

An interesting court case was held, on Wednesday 13th October 1982, at Thame Magistrates Court.

Allan Ruxton of Thame, had been stopped several times by Police for displaying the number plate RUX 10N, with two bolts above the "1" to give the appearance of a "T", making the number plate look like "RUXTON". The Police gave him time to change the plate on his MGB GT but Mr. Ruxton ignored their warnings and was prosecuted.

There were two charges, firstly that he failed to display a distinguishable registration mark and secondly that the registration mark was not of a character as prescribed by the regulations.

Prosecutor, Mr. Peter Ross opened proceedings by stating that Mr. Ruxton had acquired a number plate of a personal variety, to which he had made an amendment which rendered the plate not easily distinguishable as RUX 10N. He admitted that there wasn't any great law on this matter but nevertheless it was not being treated as a petty offence. He called the first Police witness, W.P.C. Sweeney and asked how far away she was, before she realised it was RUX 10N, to which she replied, "very, very close". The defence solicitor, Robert Wise, opened by asking her "did you say, you've got one week to remove those nuts or I'll nick you", to which she emphatically replied, "no".

The second Police witness, P.C. Evans told the court that he was five yards away before he realised it was RUX 10N. The Officer said that he warned Mr. Ruxton on several occasions, and on the 21st June he cautioned him and advised him that he would be reported for the two offences. He also provided two photographs of the number plate that he had taken.

The third Police witness, P.C. Oliver, told the court that he was 100 yards away, when he realised the plate was RUX 10N and not RUX-TON. His estimate of the distance was a considerable difference to the other two witnesses. After all, if a plate is distinguishable at

Allan Ruxton with RUX 10N

100 yards, surely the defence have proved their case!

The prosecution claimed that the layout of the plate was not as prescribed in the Road Vehicles Licensing Regulations 1971. The distance between the "X" and the "1" did not comply. However, as none of the Police Officers had measured the distances, the Magistrates agreed with the Defence, that there was no case to answer and dismissed it.

Continuing with the matter of the plate not being distinguishable, Mr. Ruxton claimed that he had consulted two Police Officers as to the legality of the plate and that neither had categorically stated that it constituted an offence. Both Officers were called as defence witnesses. Sergeant Jones and Superintendent Blowfield, both denied leading him to believe that the plate conformed with the law.

The actual number plate in question was produced in evidence. One couldn't help thinking that the Magistrates were becoming increasingly concerned with the complexities of the case and the time involved, they had listened for over an hour, to five Police witnesses and reams of legal jargon describing how a car number plate should be displayed. All this for a few bolts! They examined the plate for several minutes, appearing to admire Mr. Ruxton's ingenuity.

The defending solicitor then claimed that there was nothing in the regulations to say where the bolts had to be placed, to fix the plate to the vehicle and as there were so few people with the surname Ruxton, the positioning of the bolts, had in fact made the plate MORE distinguishable.

The prosecution didn't agree, "come on Mr. Ruxton, you bought that number plate specifically to look like you surname". He smiled and had to agree.

The case had lasted a total of one and a half hours, although it took the Magistrates just a few minutes to decide that Allan Ruxton was guilty of not displaying a distinguishable registration mark. He was fined £15 with £30 costs.

Martin Davey pictured before his court case, with 4434 MD on his Triumph car.

When I met Martin Davey at the 1982 Longleat Car Numbers Rally, I didn't really believe his story that he was using the registration number 1V 1V 111 IV MD (instead of 4434 MD) on his car on the public highway. However, a few months later it became clear that he was telling the truth, as he had been summoned to appear at Swindon Magistrates Court for using the Roman numerals instead of the ordinary Arabic characters. The Police claimed that the use of Roman numerals constituted an offence under the Road Vehicles (Registration & Licensing) Regulation 1971. Schedule 2, section 17, states that the number plates must comply with the pattern as laid down in that Schedule. The patterns clearly show Arabic figures (1,2,3, etc...).

I was rather surprised that Inspector Robert Evans (Prosecuting), didn't point out that the Roman numerals for 4434 are not 1V 1V 111 1V but are 1VCDXXX1V. Graham Young, Defending, claimed that the Regulations didn't actually specify the characters that should be displayed on the plate. The Magistrates adjourned the case for three weeks and then on Monday 7th February 1983, Martin Davey was fined £20. There was no appeal.

If Roman numerals had been permissible, many new combinations would have been added to the list of potentially interesting marks, such as 6TAL which would read, "V1TAL" and 100 AR would read "CAR".

Martin Davey may just have been a little hard done by, because a case involving the style of lettering had already been won in 1979, by Anthony P. Dagnan of Birmingham, who was prosecuted for having italic style lettering on his number plates (329 APD).

Mr. Dagnan was stopped by Police in Northfield, Birmingham, in December 1978 and was reported for illegal lettering, However, when the case finally came to court in May 1979, the prosecution could offer no evidence and the case was dismissed. Mr. Richard Jilkes appearing for Mr. Dagnan, pointed out that the regulations were devised to ensure that lettering was correctly arranged and had the correct background. The regulations did not cover the style of lettering he claimed.

An overjoyed Mr. Dagnan, subsequently purchased 222 APD and displayed both plates with "italic" style lettering. Once again he was prosecuted and won his case.

Mr Dagnan claims that he has confirmation from the Department of Transport that his style of plates are legal. He says, "the only plate I could find in 1976, was 329 APD, which is about as distinctive as coal in Newcastle. I therefore looked for a legal way of making it distinctive and I found one."

The danger is that "smart alecs" will go too far and force legislation that will spoil the harmless fun, enjoyed by Mr. Dagnan. It should, of course, be remembered that primarily, registration numbers are a legal requirement to enable every vehicle to have a unique and easily distinguishable identification. It is important that the Police are not hampered by having to decipher every number of every vehicle that passes by.

Size of Number Plates

NUMBER plate sizes are determined by U.K. laws – The Road Vehicle (Registration & Licensing) Regulations 1971 and subsequent amendments. The regulations state that the sizes, other than for bicycles, invalid vehicles or pedestrian controlled vehicles, shall be as follows:-

1. Each letter or figure shall be 3.1/8"(80 mm) high, 2¼ (57 mm) wide and have a 9/16"(14 mm) stroke width. (Except for the figure 1 or letter I).
2. The space between each letter or figure shall be 7/16"(11 mm).
3. On a single line registration, the space between the group of letters and the group of figures shall be 1.5/16"(33 mm).
4. On a two line registration, the space between the upper and lower line shall be ¾" (19 mm).
5. The space between the letter or figures and the edge of the plate shall be at least 7/16 " (11 mm).

The effect of these regulations is that the minimum size of plate for a full seven figure registration is 20.1/8"x 4"(551 mm x 102 mm) for a single line format and 11.3/16" x 7.7/8 (284 mm x 200 mm) for a two line format. In practise, most manufacturers have a ¼"(6 mm) bead round the standard size plates.

Although current regulations state Imperial measurements, metric equivalents are given in brackets.

The 1971 regulations also state that registration marks shall be formed of white, silver, or light grey letter on a black background, unless the plate is reflective, in which case the letters must be black on a white front plate or yellow rear plate.

Motor Cycles

Front number plates are no longer required on motor cycles.

1. Each letter or figure (except for 1 or I) shall be 2½"(64mm) high, 1¾"(44 mm) wide and have a ⅜"(10 mm) stroke width.
2. The space between each letter of figure shall be ⅜" (10 mm).
3. The upper, lower and side margins shall be at least ⅜"(10 mm)
4. The space between the lines of letters and figures shall be ½"(13 mm).

The effect of these regulations is that the minimum size of plate for a two line registration is 8.⅞"(225 mm) x 6¼"(159 mm) and for three lines, 6¾"(171 mm) x 9¼"(235 mm).

THE Number-plate on Wayne Davies's white Rolls-Royce Silver Shadow was just a bit TOO SEXY for the South Wales Police and so landed him in court on Thursday, 13th November, 1980.

Although Mr. Davies, 43-year-old proprietor of a Bedwas car-hire and sales business, has been offered up to £10,000 for the number-plate – 2 5EXY – he will not part with his prized possession.

For the saucy Rolls is in great demand from couples who want to add a little spice to their wedding-day pictures. The car has even made appearances at Buckingham Palace garden parties.

And no one objected to the white Rolls's message until late one May night when Mr. Davies was stopped by a police patrol car on Western Avenue. Cardiff.

After measurements of the number-plate were taken Police-Constable Richard Hill told Mr. Davies that it was illegal. "Oh, no it's not. You had better report me and we will have it out in court," he replied.

So Wayne Davies, equipped with number-plate and solicitor, appeared at Cardiff Magistrates' Court to offer a "not guilty" plea, which proved successful because of a legal technicality.

"It's a slightly unusual case," said Mr. Michael Spiller, for the prosecution. "The registration does read 25 EXY but the five has been moved and it now reads 2 5EXY (Too Sexy).

Mr. Davies uses his car for business and it's a great selling point. But, unfortunately, he has contravened the regulations which set out the distance between various numbers and various letters."

Mr. Spiller said the numbers and letters must be separated by 1½ inches or one-and-five-sixteenths of an inch. But the figure 5 and the letters EXY were separated by only half-an-inch on Mr. Davies's car.

The distance between the two and the five should have been only half or seven-sixteenths of an inch according to the regulations. The distance between the two numbers was, in fact, 2¼ inches.

Mr. Rhidian Davies, for the defence, said the facts relating to the matter were not in dispute, but, he argued in his submission, the police had not put forward evidence relating to the set of rules governing the height of the numbers and letters.

According to Mr. Rhidian Davies because the police had not taken the measurements of the height of the number and figures on the registration plate when they stopped Mr. Davies they could not possibly know which "option" Mr. Davies took when he bought the car.

For, every car owner has the option of choosing one of two heights for the numbers and letters on the car's registration plate, even though the difference between the two sizes is only about one-sixteenth of an inch.

And because the police had not offered evidence on which option Mr. Davies had chosen simply because they had not measured the height of the numbers and letters, the defence had no case to answer.

"There is an area that the prosecution has not covered which is essential before the defence can answer the prosecution. I submit there is no case for the defence to answer," said Mr. Rhidian Davies.

The magistrates' Chairman Mr. J.D. Lewis, upheld the submission and the case against Mr. Davies was dismissed.

After the hearing, Mr. Davies said, "I am delighted with the outcome, I'm now going out to screw the number plates back on."

Reflective & Non-Reflective Plates

Reflective number plates have been permissible since December 1967; but under the Road Vehicles (Registration & Licensing) (Amendments) Regulations 1972, all vehicles except those listed below must have reflective number plates fitted if registered on or after 1st January 1973.

The special cases exempt from these regulations are:-

1. Vehicles having an unladen weight exceeding 3 tons being vehicles on which it is necessary to fit rear vehicle markers.
2. Vehicles which are used wholly or mainly as stage carriages.
3. The front number plate on bicycles, invalid vehicles, or pedestrian controlled vehicles.

All reflective number plates must, by law, conform to British Standard B.S. AU145a and the plates must be marked with the manufacturers name or trade mark and the British Standard number.

The Number Plate Manufacturers Association is formed to represent the majority of major manufacturers in the U.K. and states that:-

1. It is illegal to fit non-reflective plates to vehicles registered on or after 1st January 1973, except as stated above.
2. It is illegal to fit number plates with other than the correct spacing as specified.
3. Number plates shall be clear and legible and have normal shape letters and figures.

Some motorists prefer non-reflective plates and (maybe) innocently use them on post-1973 cars. It is of course, a classic way to get pulled up by the Police and that's exactly what happened to Neil Taylor of Radlett, Hertfordshire, who owns NNT 4. His car, a Volvo, was registered after 1st January 1973 and therefore, by law, should have been displaying reflective number plates. He was stopped by Police in January 1982 for the offence and was later found guilty by Hendon Magistrates. He was fined £10.

However, Mr Taylor couldn't believe the pettiness of the Law and spent approximately £1,000 in legal costs, fighting the case. He spent many hours corresponding with the Home Office and various other bodies. His pleas have not been heard, as the Law remains the same and his conviction stands.

Another case that went to Court, on the same subject, had a happier ending for the defendant. Again, in 1982, a motorist was prosecuted by the Police for not displaying reflective number plates on a 1981 Rover. However, the Police lost the case as the defendant successfully argued that the form V 317 (yes – the one that's meant to give all the information about cherished transfers to the public), as revised in March 1979, issued by the Department of Transport, clearly stated that once the transfer had been authorised, the applicant must "ensure that registration plates now on the donor vehicle are transferred to the recipient vehicle". The Defendant did exactly that, he used the old original non-reflective plates from the donor vehicle and put them on to his Rover. The case must have been referred to DVLC, as the new forms now make reference to the requirement to use reflective plates in relevant cases.

Shady Dealings

With vast amounts of money changing hands, perhaps it was inevitable that rogues would cash in on the numbers business. Let me assure you that it is a hard task to achieve success in the business and an easy way out must have proved a great temptation to a few.

The Fraud Squad are known to be investigating several serious cases. The general problem has been the resurrecting of "dead" numbers. That is, the reregistering of vehicle registration marks that that were not registered on the computer. The rogues overlooked a problem. They assumed that as a number was not allocated to a vehicle through D.V.L.C., Swansea, it was "available" for use again. However, they did not bargain for vehicles stored in garages and museums, that had not been converted from the L.T.O. registration system to the computer. Slowly but surely they are being caught out, as the rightful owners apply for registration to the computer, with supporting documents to prove their claims. National press reports have indicated that several Civil Servants from Local Vehicle Licensing Offices have been suspended from duties pending enquiries into such fraudulent dealings.

The criminal element will always provide the authorities with ammunition for changing the system. I will be the first to agree with any changes that will stamp out any openings for fraud. However, I do not agree with changes that prevent the honest applicant from changing numbers from one vehicle to another, with freedom. Such a classic example was the abolition of the retention system, that enabled registration numbers to be held in suspense after initial transfer from the donor vehicle, thus providing the applicant with a time period in which to decide the appropriate recipient vehicle. The Department of Transport claimed in August 1977, "the new conditions of transfer which have applied since January this year – were devised with a view to eliminating, or at least discouraging, abuses which had arisen in one way or another from the fact that people are willing to pay considerable sums for what are, to them, attractive registration marks. For instance, retention certificates led to many of the abuses because they were often fraudulently altered or sold to unwitting buyers as though they were transferrable. This is why they were abolished".

I can safely say that I dealt with more retention certificates in 1975-1976, than I had hot dinners, and at no time was I ever aware of someone trying to sell me or any other person a certificate. Their claim that they were often fraudulently altered could not possibly carry any weight, because the certificate issued by the Local Taxation Office, was more or less a receipt; the actual documentation appertaining to the mark, was held on file at the L.T.O., and the retention certificate would HAVE to correspond with the details held in the file. If they are claiming that the actual files were tampered with by a Civil Servant within the L.T.O., then they must have had proof and in which case I presume that the Fraud Squad would be called in to deal with such an offender. However, the activities of crooked Civil Servants should not be used as an excuse to deprive the public of the most sensible method of transfer. The whole episode underlines the petty mindedness of Civil Servants who were hell bent on disrupting the smooth transfer system and then crawling back with feeble excuses for their action.

Perhaps one of the easiest varieties of illegal trading is the simple process of removing a set of number plates from a vehicle and fixing another set, that have no relevance to that vehicle. Anyone without a basic knowledge of car numbers could be taken in by such deceit. Unfortunately, the inadequacies of D.V.L.C.,'s computer system even make it possible to obtain documents for such a vehicle. However, it should be stressed that this fraud would soon be uncovered and would present the police with very little difficulty in obtaining a prosecution against the guilty party. It could be that the financial damage had been done to the innocent party and no hope of compensation possible.

Several cases have emerged over the years of company employees and other persons, selling numbers that do not belong to them. It should be remembered that the "registered keeper" of a vehicle is not necessarily the legal owner. The warning is clearly printed on every V5 registration document. Therefore it should be checked that in the event of buying a registration number, the person selling and transferring the number, although the registered keeper, is in fact the legal owner. This type of case can be compared with someone who sells a vehicle that is subject to a hire purchase agreement, whereas he will probably be the "registered keeper", the vehicle is the property of the hire purchase company. It is up to the intending purchaser to ensure that the seller is the legal owner.

Complications can arise when an agreement is made between two parties, for the seller to retain the rights to a number plate after the vehicle has been purchased by the buyer. I do not know of any specific cases that have ended up in court; however, I have heard of many situations when such agreements are made and subsequently dishonoured. The problem is that in the eyes of the law, a registration number does not belong to a person but it belongs to a vehicle. The person who buys the vehicle has a legal obligation to continue displaying that number, unless he chooses to pay the prescribed fee to have the mark transferred to another vehicle. This has been a major problem created by the unreasonable withdrawal of the retention facility and has enabled dishonest people to cash in. The moral of this story is (until the retention system is re-instated), not to sell a vehicle before the number plate has been transferred. If it is absolutely impossible to keep the vehicle until a transfer can be arranged, a legal document should be drawn up between the two parties, stating that the number plate will be transferred back to the original owner within a specified period. Although, it should be noted that this is still not a guarantee of protection against loss of the number.

As long as the ban remains on transferring registration numbers from vehicles that are not subject to MOT/HGV/PSV testing, there will be large quantities of vehicles with interesting numbers, complete with the proper registration documentation, that will be sold to unwitting buyers, who think they will be able to transfer the number at a later date. Whilst most of these transactions may well be innocent, there are

bound to be the odd few who take advantage. The moral of this story is, make absolutely sure that the donor vehicle qualifies for transfer BEFORE you buy it.

Certain national newspapers who run registration number advertising sections warn readers to check that transfer is possible before entering into legal liability. They recommend that the form V 317 is obtained, as this details the rules governing transfer. Consequently, at the time of going to press, many people are buying what they think to be a transferrable registration mark, when it may not be. The form implies that it is possible to transfer a registration from a donor vehicle that has no MOT or tax. Some people are asking high prices for vehicles in very poor condition, merely because of the registration. Whilst again, the majority of such cases will be innocent, there are bound to be people who knowingly sell such vehicles, that have no likelihood of falling into the scope of the transfer scheme. (See the section on "Rules of Transfer" for guidance).

Inevitably, during my early years in the business I was taken for a ride or two, by clients. I had to learn the hard way and a few examples of the losses I incurred and an example of a classic shady deal was the sale of the number 11 RYD to a chap in Scotland. He told me that as he was due to travel down to London he would meet me on the Motorway and pay me the cash for the number. I agreed that this would be in order and a date and place were arranged. However, the day before the meeting, he telephoned to say that he couldn't make it and he would post the money to me. Like a fool, I completed the transfer and assumed that the money was en route. But it was not to be. Of course he claimed that he had posted it to me and he gave me several variations of how he had posted it. I was unable to issue a County Court summons because he lived in Scotland and I decided that it was not worth pursuing any other legal course for recovery.

A few months later I was told by a dealer, whom I knew to be considering me as a naive newcomer to the business, that he knew the chap and he didn't wish to get involved. It transpired that he lived a few streets away, and to this day I believe that between the two of them they successfully ripped me off.

The tighter transfer rules imposed in 1977, did achieve the elimination of "cowboy" dealers. The tough restrictions have ensured that today's leading dealers are responsible experts. They need to be, to survive. The quality of C.N.D.A., membership has considerably improved and new guidelines within the Association, really make it essential for any serious dealer to be a member. The public have an added assurance now of fair play when dealing with a member. If a dealer is not prepared to trade under the guidelines of the Association, then it is my opinion that he has something to fear. Any bona fide dealer can join the Association. It therefore makes sense, that intending purchasers should ensure that the dealer is a C.N.D.A., member before parting with any cash. Although it should be noted that the C.N.D.A., does not have a fund to deal with any member becoming bankrupt.

Year Letters

ALTHOUGH the present D.V.L.C. policy is not to issue interesting combinations with year letters, there are plenty in circulation.

When CHR 1S was due to be issued at Swindon L.V.L.O., they were inundated with requests for it. The value of the number is around £12,000 and if the present market trends continue, it will increase accordingly. Provided the Government play their cards right, there are plenty more such combinations that would create a huge revenue. Perhaps their present policy is really to store such numbers as CHRIS, for the moment, as opposed to voiding them for all time.

New possibilities have been created, with the advent of year prefix letters. In the "B" series for example the format (not DVLC), would permit-BIBLE, BIKER, BICEP, BIDDY, BIDES, BIDET, BIFFS, BINGE, BIOMAS, BIOPSY, BIOTAS, BIPED, BIRCH, BIRDS, BIRKS, BIROS, BIRTH, BISON, BITES, BITTS, BITTY, BIVVY, BINGO and BILLY.

Until 1967 the year letter changed in January. Since then at the request of the motor manufacturers, it has changed in August, but this clashes with the holiday season, and the Department will be considering with the motor trade whether an alternative month might be more convenient. They will also be considering whether age letters are suitable for certain vehicles, particularly imported used vehicles and rebuilt vehicles.

No change is envisaged to the present distribution of index letters among the 53 local offices which currently register all new vehicles. Neither is change envisaged in the format of marks for diplomatic and consular vehicles or of marks for military vehicles.

The Cherished Numbers Dealers Association agreed by a majority in 1980, that reversing the suffix system would be the most suitable arrangement. However, a few dealers had presented complicated alternatives that quite frankly, whilst ingenious, could have had a damaging effect on cherished numbers.

The Minister's announcement was welcomed by most cherished number owners. As well as preserving the maximum seven character format, the prefix letter undoubtedly adds extra value to the much older pre-1963 plate.

It is possible to transfer a number with a year letter from one vehicle to another, provided that the recipient vehicle is not older than the year letter suggests. In other words, a registration with a "Y" suffix could not be transferred to a vehicle registered before 1st August, 1982.

DVLC do seem to make a habit of creating rules to suit themselves and to curb infiltration of non-suffix marks to the market. Whilst on the one hand they apply the code of not permitting vehicles to be up-dated via cherished transfer, they insist that replacement marks issued to donor vehicles after cherished transfer, should (in cases of pre-1963 registered vehicles), be allocated a year suffix, which is generally a "B" suffix letter. Therefore, if a donor vehicle is, for example a 1957 registered car, DVLC up-date the age by seven years, by putting a 1964 suffix mark on it. The reason behind such irrational bureaucracy is, (and they admit it), to prevent the replacement mark having any commercial value.

There is a market for registration numbers with year letters, although it is limited to name numbers (e.g. ROY, PAM, MAX), and single digit registrations. (e.g. AMG 1H, ALS 3C). These values are considerably lower than registrations without year letters.

From the 1st August 1983, the Department of Transport banned the issue of all registration numbers between 1 and 20. Therefore, you will not see a registration with an "A" prefix and the number 1. Their reasoning behind this one is that the LVLO's are inundated with requests for registration numbers with low digits, especially a number one.

The prefix letter format =

A	123	BCD
year letter	serial number	B= serial letter.
		CD= index letters of the office at which the vehicle is first registered.

Number Insurance

Registration number insurance was a phenomenon of the late seventies. As more and more numbers became valuable assets, it made good sense to insure them. At the time, a number could be lost forever, if the vehicle was stolen and never recovered. Insurance companies jumped at the chance to offer policies covering such loss.

Many people believe that their normal car policy will cover the loss of the value of the registration mark. This is just not so, in the majority of cases.

In January 1983 the rules were changed and it has now become possible to get the stolen mark back (for transfer to any other vehicle in the scope of the scheme), once it has been registered as stolen by the police and DVLC for a period of five years.

Some people are still insuring against such risk and naturally the insurance companies are willing to take the premiums. The idea is that the insurance is paid out if the vehicle is stolen and after the five years have elapsed, the registration becomes the property of the insurance company. They can then sell it on the open market or offer it back to the original owner.

In my opinion, it seems a pretty safe bet for the insurance company. They collect the premium (which incidentally, hasn't decreased since the risk was so considerably reduced), and run the chance of being left with an increasing asset. Of course they would lose out if the market took a turn for the worse, but if the past ten years are anything to go by, the values will keep rising.

Although five years are a long time to wait, it is at least comforting to know that the number will eventually be returned to you. This period has been promised to be reduced progressively. A period of twelve months would be a more suitable length of time.

It is not exactly a lot to ask for, bearing in mind that a thief with the intelligence of a dehydrated cabbage would be hardly likely to continue using the vehicle for longer than twelve months.

There are a few ways that a number can be lost.

Firstly, if the donor vehicle chassis number is found to be missing or incorrect at the time of transfer inspection. Secondly, if the vehicle is destroyed to such an extent that the chassis number could not be identified. Thirdly, if a discrepancy occurs in the transfer application, DVLC reserve the right to void the number. An example would be the applicant forging a signature on the form V317. These three cases are not likely to occur if intelligence is used. Whether or not such reasons for loss of the number would be covered by the insurance policy, would of course, depend on the individual company. The advice, therefore, is to establish exactly what is being covered. (Loss could also be caused by industrial action).

If you do insist on insuring your number, you are likely to be asked to supply a written valuation for the number from a CNDA member.

The first stolen mark to be re-allocated under the new rules, was believed to be FGR 1. The original car, a Triumph Herald was stolen from Franklin G. Roberts (pictured below) in March 1975 and was never recovered. In May 1983, DVLC permitted Mr. Roberts, to use the registration mark, on his latest vehicle, a 1970 Ford Cortina 1600 GT.

Statistics

One of the most interesting statistics must surely be how much the Government make out of each cherished transfer. On the 26th January 1983, Sir Hector Monro (MP for Dumfries, tabled a question in the Commons, asking for a breakdown in costs. Lynda Chalker MP, for the Government, said that 1982 costs were about £20 – £25. The cost in 1977 was about £10 – £15.

Profits for the Government are as follows:-
1977 – 78 £1,120,000
1978 – 79 £1,300,000
1979 – 80 £1,520,000
1980 – 81 £1,390,000
1981 – 82 £1,770,000
1982 – 83 £2,030,000
(projected)

The figures prove a constant rate of growth in the industy, although the rise cannot be termed as spectacular. The figures were supplied by Lynda Chalker and only reflect transfer fees. Taxes will have netted another huge revenue for the Government.

In 1980, DVLC claim that they processed 33,500 cherished transfers and in September of that year, the annual census of licensed vehicles, showed that 15,727,000 cars and vans were licensed. Approximately one in 470 had a cherished transfer. It is estimated that 200,000 vehicles have distinctive/personalised plates. At that rate, in 1980, one in 78 cars are estimated to be carrying them.

VALUES

The charts below show a cross section of numbers that I have been involved with over the years. The amount in the first column is the advertised asking price at the date shown. The second price is my valuation at February 1983. The figures prove that whilst values have levelled off in the past few years, most numbers prove a healthy investment.

Registration Number	Advertised Price in December 1975	February 1983 Value	Total % Increase	Increase per annum
JBL 9	£350	£820	134%	19%
260 BMW	£120	£550	358%	51%
567 FG	£225	£450	100%	14%
11 SRL	£150	£820	446%	64%
860 D	£150	£350	133%	19%
SCO 1	£1500	£2200	47%	7%
RNM 2	£450	£850	89%	13%
3857 DH	£95	£350	268%	38%
PAM 579	£120	£550	358%	51%

Registration Number	Advertised price in January 1981	February 1983 Value	Total % Increase	Increase per annum
492 ANN	£620	£720	16%	8%
222 BRW	£520	£550	6%	3%
JAM 602	£420	£520	24%	12%
805 LG	£320	£380	19%	9.5%
NRP 8	£820	£820	0%	0%
3721 PG	£200	£320	60%	30%
954 NT	£320	£420	31%	15.5%
OWV 63	£150	£190	26%	13%
569 EWV	£95	£140	47%	23.5%
216 BMW	£520	£550	19%	9.5%

The Politicians

As the public interest in personalised plates has rapidly increased over the past ten years, so has the political interest.

In 1977 the Labour Government, represented by John Horam MP (Under Secretary of State for Transport), declared that it was right and proper that a good socialist profit should be made from cherished transfers. They promptly increased the transfer fee by over 900% from £5 to £50. Their action made it more difficult for the not so well off motorist to enjoy the pleasures of owning a distinctive registration number. They also introduced harsh transfer rules to complement the inflated fee. Transport Minister, William Rodgers was unrepentant, he was adamant that it would remain difficult to carry out a cherished transfer. Ironically, he later formed an alliance with a Liberal Party leader, David Steel, who himself indulged in the harmless fun of owning a personalised number plate.

When the Conservatives came to power in 1979, they promised to change the transfer rules. Two years later, Secretary of State for Transport, Norman Fowler (pictured, issued a Consultation Paper, that proposed sweeping changes, that included consideration to the return of the retention system, (without such a system every motorist is blackmailed into acquiring a second vehicle before he has disposed of the first one, each time he transfers the registration mark). He also proposed to end restrictions of transfers between different classes of vehicles. He wanted to reduce donor vehicle inspections between 70% and 80%. Mr Fowler's proposals were most welcomed, it was a long awaited return to sanity. However, whilst the back room bureaucrats were employing delaying tactics, the job of Transport Secretary went to the docile David Howell. He delegated his Under-Secretary, Lynda Chalker, (pictured), the job of sorting out the cherished transfer mess. She performed her duty with all the finesse of a dancing elephant. She closed her mind to public opinion and refused to introduce the best of Norman Fowler's "promised land". In

Rt Hon Norman Fowler. Appointed Minister of Transport on 7 May 1979.

January 1983, as the Conservative first term of office was reaching its end, she introduced a few virtually inconsequential changes to the transfer system and at the same time, closed the door on thousands of potential cherished transfers. The main changes were the ending of the three months waiting rule, stolen marks could now be transferred again by the rightful owner (but only after being recorded as stolen for five years) and people acquiring a registration for the first time, didn't need to have extra owners on their V5 registration documents. She abolished the right to transfer marks from over thirty classes of vehicles, (the opposite of Norman Fowler's proposals).

When the Conservatives were returned to power for a second term of office, a shake up of

123

Ministers, put Tom King in the Transport driving seat. I was particularly pleased with this, as his home is a ten minutes drive from mine. If he didn't show more sympathy than the previous management, it wouldn't be far to go, with my placards.

Despite making promises of great changes, the Conservatives have let all owners of cherished numbers, down. Lynda Chalker even had the cheek to claim that her new improved rules, made life much easier for the ordinary motorist. The changes she referred to are there for everyone to see. They make very little difference to the ordinary motorist, however, her mind has been closed for her by her advisors at DVLC Swansea and only continued pressure will eventually result in a fair and workable system, that is free from bureaucracy and abuse.

I have no doubt that all the real decisions rest with DVLC, Swansea, and in my opinion all politicians are their puppets. So much for democracy!

Some Members of Parliament own cherished numbers, notably David Steel, Sir Hector Monro, Anthony Berry, and Kenneth Warren.

The Thatcher family were the proud owners of DT 3, until Margaret's claim to fame, when security advisors, forced Dennis to sell the plate. It is now owned by a Yorkshire business man.

By tradition the MP for Hastings has maintained a car number plate bearing the digits 1066 and of course most Local Councils sport distinctive registrations on official cars.

Lynda Chalker M.P.

How Registration Numbers are Valued

MANY people comment at how much a seemingly undesirable registration has been priced at. "Who on earth would want that? they say.

Basically, registrations are valued by two factors. Firstly, the rarity of the combination. For example: Mr. A. M. Jones sees AMJ 8 advertised at £750 and he also sees 9 AMJ advertised at £450. The first combination was issued in 1936 making it very rare, as there are few 1936 cars left on the road, let alone ones carrying AMJ registrations. 9 AMJ was issued in 1960, hence not so rare and far cheaper.

Secondly, popularity of initials is a major factor when it comes to valuing. Believe it or not, our example, Mr. Jones does NOT have a popular surname initial. Statistically, the "J" is way down the list. However, Mr. Brown (surname initial "B") is at the top of the list. Obviously "O", "U", "X" and "Y" are not popular in either surname or first name initials. There are always exceptions to the rule and in this case, an example is the combination "ROY". This being a name the value is great owing to it being popular and the "O" & "Y" are not considered initials.

Some dealers will rate single letter registrations, e.g. A 4286, far more than others. The majority of these, are very rare issues, some of which date back as far as 1904. However, despite the obvious value for rarity, it must be argued that the market for such numbers is diminished because people would rather spend considerable amounts of money on acquiring their initials.

Makes and models of cars can have value added to them if a suitable registration is transferred to it. For example an XJ plate would suit a Jaguar XJ series and a VW plate on a Volkswagen. SAB 1 has been spotted on a Ford, it would, of course, be far more at home on a Saab.

Car Models can also influence prices. For example AJB 351 would not be as desirable as AJB 924 if it was transferred to a Porsche 924, hence the latter would be more valuable.

With the exception of the classic "TR" single digit registration numbers, probably the most unique pair of TR registrations in existence are 1971 TR and 1972 TR.

The cars were first registered in 1971 and 1972 respectively and the registration numbers were purchased in 1979/1980, coinciding with the cars being taken off the road for total rebuilds. In this case, the year of first registration adds value.

In the early days, I didn't note the significance of the number 911 and the famous Porsche model. Consequently, OPR 911 went for a song. I had purchased the number on a Lambretta

125

scooter and was happy to take a £40 profit. I sold this superb number for just £55. I realised my mistake as soon as the phone started ringing, the morning the advertisement appeared.

An astute employee of Porsche Cars in Great Britain, was the first to phone. Fortunately, for him, I am not in the business of gazumping, so in November 1975, the plate was transferred to a brand new Porsche 911. At least the number went to the best possible home. It has been used on Porsche demonstration cars ever since. The most recent, at the time of going to press, is the model 911 pictured above. The car firm were delighted to send me the photograph with their compliments. Lady Luck certainly shined on them, (thank heavens it wasn't POR 911!)

Another registration number that "slipped away" for a song, was 5 KUO, also in November 1975. I was advertising the registration for just £95. A gentleman phoned, telling me that his name was Stanley Kuo and that 5 KUO would be the perfect registration for him. He had a dental practice in London.

Of course, he shouldn't have said that his name was Kuo, as I just might have been an unscrupulous person who would push the price sky high on hearing such information.

He purchased the number at the advertised price and was absolutely delighted. I asked if he would mind driving up to Wiltshire to show me the plate and to have a photograph taken. He agreed and a few weeks after the transfer, he came up with his absolutely charming family, stayed a few hours and after the photograph was taken, the dentist with his "doctored" 5 KUO, drove the 100 miles back home.

The valuation of a personalised number is not as simple as looking through advertisements to find one of a similar appearance. It is a professionally acquired skill that is gained from many years of constant dealing in registrations. Apart from statistics of popularity of initials and rarity of issue, perhaps the most important factor, is the current market trend. It is no use having a rare registration mark for sale at an inflated price, if there is no potential market for it.

Inevitably, private advertisers tend to grossly over-price their registration numbers, when advertising in the national press. If only people would spend a few pounds obtaining a professional valuation, they could save themselves money in the long run, by reducing the amount of advertising needed to sell the number.

Advertising

ADVERTISING could be responsible for the enormous increase in popularity of personalised car number plates, over the last decade. If entrepreneurs had not risked their cash in expensive advertising, the market would be non-existent. Instead, as businesses have expanded, so has the advertising. As well as the trade, the market place has been used to considerable advantage by the private individual.

The original "shop window" for selling car numbers was The Sunday Times. However, numerous industrial problems over the years have forced dealers and the public to seek an alternative medium to sell plates. That alternative was the Exchange & Mart and over the past years has rivalled The Sunday Times in the competition for advertising. Other national papers have all tried to jump in on the action, but without success. These are notably, The Times, The Guardian, The Telegraph, Sunday Telegraph and The Observer.

The only specialist paper in the car numbers field, is Car Numbers Monthly and is naturally an obvious medium for selling numbers. Dealers have been impressed with results and each month sees a trickle of private advertisers either selling or wanting to acquire plates, through the paper.

It is believed that the only firm to advertise on Independent Television, is Elite Registrations. Using a colour slide with voice over and specially recorded music, the advertisements have created a reasonable amount of interest.

When advertising a car number privately it is usually best to sell the plate without the vehicle. The reason being that the majority of people wanting to buy numbers, firstly, want them "yesterday" and secondly do not want to go to all the trouble and expense of acquiring a second vehicle. These people usually have an expensive or distinctive vehicle and the last thing they want outside the house is an undesirable motor car.

Private advertisers often make the mistake of selling the number with the vehicle or waiting until they are ready to sell the car, then place the advertisement to sell the number seperately. Licensing Offices rarely carry out immediate transfers, therefore many motorists do not obtain the best prices, simply because they have left it too late.

Advertisements can sometimes include the same registration number being offered by several dealers and at varying prices. These cases are generally when the number is sold on a commission basis and the vendor has instructed more than one selling agent. Varying commission charges often result in fluctuating selling prices. Searching through telephone directories and offering compatible registrations, can work, but requires considerable patience.

Rules of Transfer

A problem of the last six years, has been the fact that Local Vehicle Licensing Office staff are not always fully conversant with the rules of cherished transfer. It isn't exactly surprising, given the amount of changes in procedure, and staff changes at the offices.

In early 1983 even the form V317, that is supposedly meant to contain accurate information how to transfer a registration mark, couldn't get it right. Despite the form being four pages of A4 size paper, the Dept., of Transport failed miserably to use the available space to explain the complexities of their own rules.

Naturally they had an excuse, a D.O.T., spokesman told me that the form was an experiment. In practise it had confused the public and LVLO staff, for over six months.

At the time of going to press, the set of transfer rules are as follows. They are not likely to be changed in the near future and they have been checked with DVLC Swansea, for total accuracy.

To transfer a registration mark form one vehicle to another, firstly obtain the form V 317 from any Local Vehicle Licensing Office.

The latest from V 317 (dated "Revised March 1983). was released in June 1983. It is an improvement to the previous forms but still falls a long way short of explaining the intricacies of cherished transfer. Pages 1 and 2 of the form, set out the D.O.T., explanations of the scheme in twelve sections. Where necessary I have added my own explanation in the form of a "GUIDE". If you are transferring a registration number as a donor or recipient, or both, you would be well advised to follow the "GUIDE" carefully.

1 How do I transfer my registration mark to another vehicle?

Apply to the Department of Transport by filling in the form. But please read the rest of the leaflet first.

2 Where do I take or send the form?

To any Local Vehicle Licensing Office. For the address ask at a post office or look in your phone book under 'Transport, Department of'.

2 GUIDE: Although you are at liberty to deal with any LVLO, a few of them may not deal with you, if you are taking the donor vehicle to them for inspection, on a trailer, because of accomodation problems at the office premises. If the donor vehicle is immobile or not roadworthy, you would be advised to inform the LVLO that it will be arriving on a trailer. (Addresses are in this book).

3 What else should I take or send?

The registration document (V5) for the donor vehicle **(the vehicle which carries the mark to be transferred).**

The registration document (V5) for the recipient vehicle **(the vehicle which will receive the mark). But if** the receiving vehicle is new, take instead your application for first registration, form V55.

A test certificate for each vehicle that requires one. (Although either vehicle may not have a certificate because of its age it must belong to a class of vehicle that normally requires MOT or HGV testing. If a vehicle is of a type that does not normally require testing, such as agricultural machines, milk floats, then it cannot take part in a transfer).

The licence disc or a completed licence application form for the donor vehicle and the receiving vehicle. But if it is inconvenient or you are posting your application, don't send the discs. Instead fill in the expiry dates in the spaces provided on the form, the Local Vehicle Licensing Office will later need to see the discs for checking.

The current fee (£80 at the time of printing).

3 GUIDE: Before you send the registration document V5, ensure that the chassis or frame number of the donor vehicle EXACTLY corresponds with that on your vehicle. ANY discrepancy may result in the failure of the inspection and the subsequent loss of the number. Although the recipient vehicle is rarely inspected to ensure that the chassis/frame number corresponds with that on the vehicle, it is ESSENTIAL that you check it. The recipient

vehicle will become the donor vehicle next time the cherished number is transferred, therefore any discrepancy should be notified to DVLC in writing to; The Policy (Vehicles) Section, DVLC, Swansea, SA6 7JL. You are advised to retain a copy of such a letter and to post the original via "recorded delivery". As the requirement for inspection is promised to be progressively reduced, the donor and recipient vehicle chassis/frame numbers should be continued to be inspected by YOU, to ensure that they are correct. DVLC and the Government have a history of changing their minds over such policy and therefore a donor vehicle inspection could be called for at any time. However, at the time of going to press, all donor vehicles are subject to inspection. If the receiving vehicle (recipient) is brand new, make sure that you obtain the form V55 from your supplying garage, well before you expect to take delivery of the vehicle. Most LVLO's are taking between two and three weeks to arrange an inspection of the donor vehicle. You will not be able to legally drive the new vehicle on the road with the transferred mark and licence disc, until the donor side of the transfer has been approved by the LVLO.

A test certificate must be produced (where appropriate), however, it need not be current if the licence remains current at the time of transfer application. After 30th September 1983, vehicles that do not require testing, such as agricultural machines, cannot take part in the transfer scheme.

The donor V5 need not be registered in the name of the transfer applicant. If it is in the previous keeper's name, the new keeper will need to fill in the changes section before transfer can take place. Also the recipient vehicle does not need to be registered in the applicant's name, although in such cases, the recipient applicant must fill in the changes section of the V5 before adding it to the full transfer application WARNING: if you licence the vehicle prior to the transfer you are liable to have the V5 sent to DVLC for up-dating and a transfer of the cherished mark will not be possible until the new V5 reaches you.

What happens next?

The Local Vehicle Licensing Office will inspect the donor vehicle at a time and place it decides. The Office may also wish to inspect the other vehicle. If the Office agrees to the transfer it will send you a V351 form which explains when you can change the plates and what to do next.

When will my new registration documents arrive?

Within 6-8 weeks of approval by the Local Licensing Office. If they don't arrive by then, write to the Vehicle Enquiry Unit, DVLC, Swansea, SA6 7JL or phone Swansea (0792) 72134.

5 GUIDE: When the new document arrives from DVLC, Swansea, this can be taken as proof that there have been no objections to the transfer, after reference to the central record. WARNING: even if the LVLO approves the transfer and permits you to fix new number plates, the transfer can still be rejected by DVLC if there is a discrepancy.

6 When can I transfer my registration mark again?

When you have received your new registration documents.

7 What if my vehicle with the registration mark has been stolen?

You can apply for the transfer only if your vehicle has been recorded as stolen at the Driver and Vehicle Licensing Centre (DVLC) Swansea for five years. Apply to the Cherished Transfer Section, DVLC, Swansea SA99 1AR for consideration.

7 GUIDE: Applications to transfer stolen marks are also considered by DVLC if the vehicle has been recorded as stolen by the police for a period of five years. Certain vehicles were not recorded at DVLC, prior to them being stolen.

8 What if the donor vehicle has failed its test?

If the donor vehicle has failed its MOT or HGV test and therefore cannot be licensed, you may still apply to transfer the registration mark. But in these circumstances you must send your application direct to the Cherished Transfer Section, DVLC, Swansea SA99 1AR for special consideration. Please enclose a letter giving any further relevant information.

8 GUIDE: DVLC claim that there is no discrimination between applications from the public and dealers. They are looking for vehicles that have been registered for approximately two years or more to the applicant and that have been licensed at some stage whilst the applicant has been the keeper. They are not encouraging people to acquire unlicensed vehicles because of an attractive registration mark. REMEMBER: if the donor vehicle cannot be licensed you have NO GUARANTEE of transfer.

9 May I transfer a mark to or from a motor-cycle or moped?

You may transfer a registration mark from a motorcycle or moped to any vehicle which is currently tested and licensed including another motorcycle or moped. You are not allowed to transfer a mark from any other type of vehicle to a motorcycle or moped.

9 GUIDE: As explained elsewhere in this book, DVLC claim that transfers to mopeds and motor-cycles cause road safety problems and are frowned on by the Police. What they really mean, is that such transfers are a means of easily storing a registration number until a suitable recipient car is available. At the time of going to press, this petty minded bureaucracy still prevails, however, it is liable to be changed, if I get my way.

10 How do I acquire a registration mark?

A registration mark may only be transferred from an existing vehicle. But under the new rules, you don't have to buy and register the vehicle that carries the mark. Instead fill in the attached form after reading the leaflet. Then ask the keeper of the vehicle which carries the mark you are buying to sign the form on the back in the space shown. He or she will be asked to produce the vehicle for inspection. But before buying the mark read the other notes on the form.

10 GUIDE: If you acquire a vehicle with the registration number of your choice make sure that the number is really registered to that vehicle before parting with your cash. If you are buying only the registration mark from an unknown person, make sure that the number is trans-ferrable. Most reputable dealers are members of the Cherished Numbers Dealers Association (C.N.D.A.), and are bound by a strict code of conduct.

11 Who do I contact if I want further information?

Telephone a Local Vehicle Licensing Office. Look in your phone book under 'Transport, Department of'.

11 GUIDE: Most LVLO's are instructed to rotate the duties of staff, consequently a member of the staff may not be fully conversant with the rules of cherished transfer. If anyone should give you information that conflicts with the details in this book, you can write to me for advice, please enclose a large stamped addressed envelope. Unfortunately, telephone enquiries cannot be dealt with. The address to write to is; P.O. Box 1, Bradford-On-Avon, Wiltshire, BA15 1YQ.

Notes to the form:-

The 'keeper' means the person registered as the keeper of the vehicle on the Registration Document (V5). The keeper normally keeps or uses the vehicle but might not be the legal owner. The keeper (not the agent or dealer) must sign the form.

Transfers are now permitted to and from vehicles that are subject to HGV and PSV testing,.

A number can be transferred to a vehicle that is the subject of customs restriction.

Once a vehicle is exported the number cannot be transferred, however, if the same vehicle is brought back to the U.K., application can be made to re-register the number as used on the vehicle, prior to exportation, at no extra cost.

A transfer will not be permitted if the registration mark it is proposed to transfer was not assigned by U.K., authorities.

A transfer will not be permitted if the mark it is proposed to transfer bears a year suffix or prefix letter that was issued in a year after that in which the proposed recipient vehicle was first registered. (In other words, it is not possible to update a vehicle by means of transferring a registration number with a year letter).

If either vehicle does not have a registration document, a duplicate can be obtained by completing the form V62, although a transfer cannot take place until the V5 arrives from DVLC.

Miscellaneous Information

This section endeavours to cover points not raised elsewhere in this book.

THE REGULATIONS GOVERNING CHERISHED TRANSFERS are contained in:-

(1) The Road Vehicles (Registration and Licensing) Regulations 1971.
(2) The Road Vehicles (Registration and Licensing (Amendment) Regulations (No. 2) 1976 SI No. 2089.
(3) The Road Vehicles (Registration and Licensing (Amendment) Regulations 1977 SI No. 230.

Copies of these Regulations are available from HMSO book shops.

AFTER TRANSFER the donor vehicle is given a new number relevant to the year of manufacture, unless it is pre-1963, when all replacement marks are given year letters. The recipient vehicle's original number is made void for all time. The donor vehicle can be kept on the road or scrapped after transfer.

SWAPPING NUMBERS is not permitted. Only one transfer can be carried out at a time.

MAN REGISTRATIONS are reserved for the Isle of Man and are not transferrable.

J REGISTRATIONS. The prefix letter J and up to five digits are Jersey issue and cannot be transferred. (Except early Durham issues).

Q REGISTRATIONS (Prefix letter), are used in situations when the year of an un-registered vehicle cannot be identified, because of lack of documentary evidence. Special non-year letter marks allocated by DVLC to previously non-recorded registrations at Swansea after 30th November 1983, will not be transferrable.
Other registrations with "Q" followed by another letter, denote a temporarily imported vehicle. These marks are issued by the Automobile Association and the Royal Automobile Club. They are not transferrable.

ALL DIGIT REGISTRATION NUMBERS are not transferrable. They are issued and used in Guernsey. The plates are the same layout as DVLC issue (but up to 5 digits), and can often be seen when temporarily imported.

Local Vehicle Licensing Offices Addresses

ENGLAND

Birmingham – St. Martin's House, Bullring, Birmingham.

Bournemouth – Tregonwell Court, 118 Commercial Road, Bournemouth, BH2 5LN

Brighton – PO Box 357, Circus House, New England Road, Brighton, BN1 1DH

Bristol – Colston House, Colston Street, Bristol, BS1 5AH

Carlisle – 23 Portland Square, Carlisle

Chelmsford – Globe House, New Street, Chelmsford, CM1 1LA

Chester – Norroy House, Nun's Road, Chester, CH1 2ND

Coventry – Greyfriars House, Greyfriars Lane, Coventry, CV1 2HB

Dudley – Churchill Precinct, Dudley, DY2 7BN

Exeter – Clifton Court, Southernhay East, Exeter, EX1 1TP

Gloucester – Elmbridge Court, Cheltenham Road, Gloucester, GL3 1JY

Guildford – Cavridy House, Lady Mead, Guildford, GU1 1BZ

Huddersfield – Kirklees House, Market Street, Huddersfield, HD1 2HR

Hull – Kingston House, Myton Street, Hull, HU1 2PE

Ipswich – P.O. Box 30, Fransciscan House Greyfriars, Ipswich.

Leeds – 24a Union Street Leeds, LS2 7JR

Leicester – County Hall, Glenfield, Leicester, LE3 8RD

Lincoln – Mill House, Brayford Side North, Lincoln, LN1 1YW

Liverpool – Corn Exchange Buildings, Fenwick Street (Entrance in Brunswick Street), Liverpool, L2 7TT

London

North East Area — 23, Balfour Road, Ilford, IG1 4HH

North West Area — 1st Floor (Building No. 2), Victoria Road (opp. Queens Mead Sports Centre), South Ruislip, HA4 0NZ

South West Area — Park House, 112-134 The Broadway, London SW19 1RH

South East Area — 12-18 Station Road, Sidcup, DA15 7EQ

Luton – 2 Dunstable Road, Luton LU1 1EB

Maidstone – Coronet House, 11 Queen Anne Road, Maidstone, ME14 1XB

Manchester – Trafford House, Chester Road, Stretford, Manchester, M32 0SL

Middlesbrough – 9th Floor, Corporation House, 73-75 Albert Road, Middlesbrough, TS1 2BP

Newcastle-upon-Tyne – Sunley House, Regent Farm Road, Newcastle-upon-Tyne, NE3 3QF

Northampton – Wootton Hall Park, Northampton, NN4 9BG

Norwich – Rouen House, Rouen Road, Norwich, NR1 1UP

Nottingham – Lambert House, Talbot Street, Nottingham, NG1 5NJ

Oxford – PO Box 66, 3-7 Cambridge Terrace, Oxford, OX1 1RW

Peterborough – 88 Lincoln Road, Peterborough, PE1 2ST

Portsmouth – 1-4 Queen Street, Portsmouth, PO1 3JD

Preston – Buckingham House, Glovers Court, Preston, PR1 4DQ

Reading – Minster House, 52-53 Minster Street, Reading, RG1 2JS

Sheffield – St. Peter's House, Hartshead, Sheffield, S1 1JX

Shrewsbury – Shire Hall, Abbey Foregate, Shrewsbury, SY2 6NG

Stoke-on-Trent – Woodhouse Street, Stoke-on-Trent, ST4 1EL

Swindon – St. Mark's School, Maxwell Street, Swindon, SN1 5DS

Taunton – Brendon House, High Street, Taunton, TA1 3NT

Truro – Eagle Star House, 74 Lemon Street, Truro, TR1 2TG

Worcester – Haswell House, St. Nicholas Street, Worcester, WR1 1NX

SCOTLAND

Aberdeen – Inverlair House, 10 West North Street, Aberdeen, AB9 1XH

Dundee – 99 Clepington Road, Dundee, DD4 7XB

Edinburgh – Pentland House, 47 Robb's Loan Edinburgh, EH14 1UW

Glasgow – 107 Bothwell Street, Glasgow, G2 7EE

Inverness – Caledonia House, 63 Academy Street, Inverness, IV1 1RP

WALES

Bangor – 1st Floor, 271 High Street, Bangor, LL57 1BX

Cardiff – 1st Floor, Hodge House, 114 St. Mary Street, Cardiff, CF1 3LF

Haverfordwest – Winch Lane, Havorfordwest, SA61 1RD

Swansea – Ty-Nant, 180 High Street, Swansea, SA1 1NA

International Identification Letters

Although not strictly enforced and in many cases abused, the international regulations governing identification letters, state that the plate must be black lettering on a white background and oval shape. Some motorists use them to identify their country of origin, whereas the vehicle maybe registered to another country. When used properly, the following list will identify the country where the vehicle is registered. It is particularly helpful to those who have an interest in foreign number plate spotting.

A	Austria	ES	El Salvador	MAL	Malaysia
ADN	Democratic Yemen	ET	Egypt	MC	Monaco
AFG	Afghanistan	F	France	MEX	Mexico
AL	Albania	FJI	Fiji	MS	Mauritius
AND	Andorra	FL	Liechtenstein	MW	Malawi
AUS	Australia	FR	Faeroe Islands	N	Norway
B	Belgium	GB	United Kingdom	NA	Antilles(Netherlands)
BD	Bangladesh	GBA	Alderney	NIC	Nicaragua
BDS	Barbados	GBG	Guernsey	NL	Holland (Netherlands)
BG	Bulgaria	GBJ	Jersey	NZ	New Zealand
BH	Belize	GBM	Isle of Man	P	Portugal
BR	Brazil	GBZ	Gibraltar	PA	Panama
BRN	Bahrain	GCA	Guatemala	PAK	Pakistan
BRU	Brunei	GH	Ghana	PE	Peru
BS	Bahamas	GR	Greece	PL	Poland
BUR	Burma	GUY	Guyana	PNG	Papua New Guinea
C	Cuba	H	Hungary	PY	Paraguay
CDN	Canada	HKJ	Jordan	RA	Argentina
CH	Switzerland	HK	Hong Kong	RB	Botswana
CI	Ivory Coast	I	Italy	RC	Taiwan
CL	Sri Lanka	IL	Israel	RCA	Central Africa
CO	Columbia	IND	India	RCB	Congo
CR	Costa Rica	IR	Iran	RCH	Chile
CS	Czechoslovakia	IRL	Republic of Ireland	RH	Haiti
CY	Cyprus	IRQ	Iraq	RI	Indonesia
D	German Federal Republic	IS	Iceland	RIM	Mauritania
DDR	German Democratic Republic	J	Japan	RL	Lebanon
DK	Denmark	JA	Jamaica	RM	Madagascar
DOM	Dominican Republic	K	Kampuchea	RMM	Mali
DY	Benin	KWT	Kuwait	RN	Niger
DZ	Algeria	L	Luxembourg	RO	Rumania
E	Spain	LAO	Laos	ROK	Korea
EAK	Kenya	LAR	Libya	RP	Philipines
EAT	Tanzania	LB	Liberia	RSM	San Marino
EAU	Uganda	LS	Lesotho	RU	Barundi
EAZ	Zanzibar	M	Malta	RWA	Rwanda
EC	Ecuador	MA	Morocco	S	Sweden
				SD	Swaziland

SF	Finland	TN	Tunisia	WD	Dominica
SGP	Singapore	TR	Turkey	WG	Grenada
SME	Surinam	TT	Trinidad & Tobago	WL	St. Lucia
SN	Senegal	U	Uruguay	WS	Western Samoa
SU	Soviet Russia	USA	United States of America	WV	St. Vincent
SWA	South West Africa	V	Vatican	YU	Yugoslavia
SY	Seychelles	VN	Vietnam	YV	Venezuela
SYR	Syria	WAG	Gambia	ZA	Republic of South Africa
T	Thailand	WAL	Sierra Leone	ZR	Zaire
TG	Togo	WAN	Nigeria	ZW	Zimbabwe

Original Licensing Authorities

The following list will enable you to establish the area of origin for any registration mark without a year letter. (Many areas have changed sequences since the introduction of DVLC, Swansea, for example FB has moved from Bath to Bristol). The list covers all registration marks without suffix or prefix letters. To establish the area of issue of a triple letter combination, ignore the first letter and use the last two. The next list will give you the year of issue of all double and single letter combinations. Unfortunately, space does not permit the massive listing required to give the triple letter years of issue, although this information is contained in a book titled "Where's It From, When Was It Issued" and can be purchased through "Car Numbers Monthly".

Examples of combinations:- 1 FBE was originally issued by the Lindsey, Lincolnshire, Authority as was FBE 1 and BE 1. SP 11 was issued by Fifeshire and GFT 1 was issued by Tynemouth.

A	London	AX	Monmouthshire	BV	Blackburn
AA	Hampshire	AY	Leicestershire	BW	Oxfordshire
AB	Worcestershire	B	Lancashire	BX	Carmarthenshire
AC	Warwickshire	BA	Salford	BY	London, Croydon
AD	Gloucestershire	BB	Newcastle upon Tyne	C	Yorkshire W.R.
AE	Bristol	BC	Leicester	CA	Denbighshire
AF	Cornwall	BD	Northamptonshire	CB	Blackburn
AG	Ayrshire	BE	Lindsey (Lincs.)	CC	Caernarvonshire
AH	Norfolk	BF	Staffordshire	CD	Brighton
AJ	Yorkshire	BG	Birkenhead	CE	Cambridgeshire &
AK	Bradford	BH	Buckinghamshire		Isle of Ely
AL	Nottinghamshire	BJ	East Suffolk	CF	West Suffolk
AM	Wiltshire	BK	Portsmouth	CG	Hampshire
AN	London West Ham	BL	Berkshire	CH	Derby
AO	Cumberland	BM	Bedfordshire	CJ	Herefordshire
AP	East Sussex	BN	Bolton	CK	Preston
AR	Hertfordshire	BO	Cardiff	CL	Norwich
AS	Nairnshire	BP	West Sussex	CM	Birkenhead
AT	Kingston upon Hull	BR	Sunderland	CN	Gateshead
AU	Nottingham	BS	Orkney	CO	Plymouth
AV	Aberdeenshire	BT	Yorkshire E.R.	CP	Halifax
AW	Shropshire	BU	Oldham	CR	Southampton

CS	Ayrshire	ES	Perthshire	GU	London
CT	Kesteven (Lincs.)	ET	Rotherham	GV	London
CU	South Shields	EU	Breconshire	GW	London
CV	Cornwall	EV	Essex	GX	London
CW	Burnley	EW	Huntingdon & Peterborough	GY	London
CX	Huddersfield			H	Middlesex
CY	Swansea	EX	Great Yarmouth	HA	Warley Smethwick
D	Kent	EY	Anglesey		
DA	Wolverhampton	F	Essex	HB	Merthyr Tydfil
DB	Stockport	FA	Burton upon Trent	HC	Eastbourne
DC	Teeside, Middlesborough	FB	Bath	HD	Dewsbury
		FC	Oxford	HE	Barnsley
DD	Gloucestershire	FD	Dudley	HF	Wallasey
DE	Pembrokeshire	FE	Lincoln	HG	Burnley
DF	Gloucestershire	FF	Merionethshire	HH	Carlisle
DG	Gloucestershire	FG	Fifeshire	HJ	Southend-on-Sea
DH	Walsall	FH	Gloucester	HK	Essex
DJ	St. Helens	FJ	Exeter	HL	Wakefield
DK	Rochdale	FK	Worcester	HM	London
DL	Isle of Wight	FL	Huntingdon & Peterborough	HN	Darlington
DM	Flintshire			HO	Hampshire
DN	York	FM	Chester	HP	Coventry
DO	Holland (Lincs.)	FN	Canterbury	HR	Wiltshire
DP	Reading	FO	Radnorshire	HS	Renfrewshire
DR	Plymouth, Devonport	FP	Rutland	HT	Bristol
DS	Peebleshire	FR	Blackpool	HU	Bristol
DT	Doncaster	FS	Edinburgh	HV	London
DU	Coventry	FT	Tynemouth	HW	Bristol
DV	Devon	FU	Lindsey (Lincs.)	HX	London Middlesex
DW	Newport (Mon.)	FV	Blackpool		
DX	Ipswich	FW	Lindsey (Lincs.)	HY	Bristol
DY	Hastings	FX	Dorset	J	Durham
E	Staffordshire	FY	Southport	JA	Stockport
EA	West Bromwich	G	Glasgow	JB	Berkshire
EB	Cambridgeshire & Isle of Ely	GA	Glasgow	JC	Caernarvonshire
		GB	Glasgow	JD	London
EC	Westmorland	GC	London	JE	Cambridgeshire
ED	Warrington	GD	Glasgow	JF	Leicester
EE	Grimsby	GE	Glasgow	JG	Canterbury
EF	Hartlepool, West Hartlepool	GF	London	JH	Hertfordshire
		GG	Glasgow	JJ	London
EG	Huntingdon & Peterborough	GH	London	JK	Eastbourne
		GJ	London	JL	Holland (Lincs.)
EH	Stoke-on-Trent Hanley	GK	London	JM	Westmorland
		GL	Bath	JN	Southend-on-Sea
EJ	Cardiganshire	GM	Motherwell & Wishaw	JO	Oxford
EK	Wigan			JP	Wigan
EL	Bournemouth	GN	London	JR	Northumberland
EM	Bootle	GO	London	JS	Ross and Cromarty
EN	Bury	GP	London	JT	Dorset
EO	Barrow-in-Furness	GR	Sunderland	JU	Leicestershire
EP	Montgomeryshire	GS	Perthshire	JV	Grimsby
ER	Cambridgeshire & Isle of Ely	GT	London	JW	Wolverhampton

JX	Halifax	MC	London	OH	Birmingham
JY	Plymouth	MD	Middlesex	OJ	Birmingham
K	Liverpool	ME	London	OK	Birmingham
KA	Liverpool	MF	London	OL	Birmingham
KB	Liverpool	MG	London	OM	Birmingham
KC	Liverpool	MH	London	ON	Birmingham
KD	Liverpool	MJ	Bedfordshire	OO	Essex
KE	Kent	MK	London	OP	Birmingham
KF	Liverpool	ML	Middlesex	OR	Hampshire
KG	Cardiff	MM	London	OS	Wigtownshire
KH	Kingston upon Hull	MN	Isle of Man	OT	Hampshire
KJ	Kent	MO	Berkshire	OU	Hampshire
KK	Kent	MP	London	OV	Birmingham
KL	Kent	MR	Wiltshire	OW	Southampton
KM	Kent	MS	Stirlingshire	OX	Birmingham
KN	Kent	MT	London	OY	London
KO	Kent	MU	London	P	Surrey
KP	Kent	MV	London	PA	Surrey
KR	Kent	MW	Wiltshire	PB	Surrey
KS	Roxburghshire	MX	London	PC	Surrey
KT	Kent	MY	Middlesex	PD	Surrey
KU	Bradford	N	Manchester	PE	Surrey
KV	Coventry	NA	Manchester	PF	Surrey
KW	Bradford	NB	Manchester	PG	Surrey
KX	Buckinghamshire	NC	Manchester	PH	Surrey
KY	Bradford	ND	Manchester	PJ	Surrey
L	Glamorganshire	NE	Manchester	PK	Surrey
LA	London	NF	Manchester	PL	Surrey
LB	London	NG	Norfolk	PM	East Sussex
LC	London	NH	Northampton	PN	East Sussex
LD	London	NJ	East Sussex	PO	West Sussex
LE	London	NK	Hertfordshire	PP	Buckinghamshire
LF	London	NL	Northumberland	PR	Dorset
LG	Cheshire	NM	Bedfordshire	PS	Zetland
LH	London	NN	Nottinghamshire		(Shetland Is.)
LJ	Bournemouth	NO	Essex	PT	Durham
LK	London	NP	Worcestshire	PU	Essex
LL	London	NR	Leicestershire	PV	Ipswich
LM	London	NS	Sutherland	PW	Norfolk
LN	London	NT	Shropshire	PX	West Suffolk
LO	London	NU	Derbyshire	PY	Yorkshire N.R.
LP	London	NV	Northamptonshire	R	Derbyshire
LR	London	NW	Leeds	RA	Derbyshire
LS	Selkirkshire	NX	Warwickshire	RB	Derbyshire
LT	London	NY	Glamorganshire	RC	Derby
LU	London	O	Birmingham	RD	Reading
LV	Liverpool	OA	Birmingham	RE	Staffordshire
LW	London	OB	Birmingham	RF	Staffordshire
LX	London	OC	Birmingham	RG	Aberdeen
LY	London	OD	Devonshire	RH	Kingston upon Hull
M	Cheshire	OE	Birmingham	RJ	Salford
MA	Cheshire	OF	Birmingham	RK	London
MB	Cheshire	OG	Birmingham		Croydon

RL	Cornwall	TR	Southampton	VU	Manchester
RM	Cumberland	TS	Dundee	VV	Northampton
RN	Preston	TT	Devon	VW	Essex
RO	Hertfordshire	TU	Cheshire	VX	Essex
RP	Northamptonshire	TV	Nottingham	VY	York
RR	Nottinghamshire	TW	Essex	W	Sheffield
RS	Aberdeen	TX	Glamorganshire	WA	Sheffield
RT	East Suffolk	TY	Northumberland	WB	Sheffield
RU	Bournemouth	U	Leeds	WC	Essex
RV	Portsmouth	UA	Leeds	WD	Warwickshire
RW	Coventry	UB	Leeds	WE	Sheffield
RX	Berkshire	UC	London	WF	Yorkshire E.R.
RY	Leicester	UD	Oxfordshire	WG	Stirlingshire
S	Edinburgh	UE	Warwickshire	WH	Bolton
SA	Aberdeenshire	UF	Brighton	WJ	Sheffield
SB	Argyllshire	UG	Leeds	WK	Coventry
SC	Edinburgh	UH	Cardiff	WL	Oxford
SD	Ayrshire	UJ	Shropshire	WM	Southport
SE	Banffshire	UK	Wolverhampton	WN	Swansea
SF	Edinburgh	UL	London	WO	Monmouthshire
SG	Edinburgh	UM	Leeds	WP	Worcestershire
SH	Barwickshire	UN	Denbighshire	WR	Yorkshire W.R.
SJ	Buteshire	UO	Devon	WS	Leith
SK	Caithness	UP	Durham	WT	Yorkshire W.R.
SL	Clackmannanshire	UR	Hertfordshire	WU	Yorkshire W.R.
SM	Dumfrieshire	US	Glasgow	WV	Wiltshire
SN	Dumbartonshire	UT	Leicestershire	WW	Yorkshire N.R.
SO	Morayshire	UU	London	WX	Yorkshire W.R.
SP	Fifeshire	UV	London	WY	Yorkshire W.R.
SR	Angus	UW	London	X	Northumberland
SS	East Lothian	UX	Shropshire	XA to XF	London
ST	Inverness-shire	UY	Worcestershire	XG	Middlesborough
SU	Kincardineshire	V	Lanarkshire	XH	London
SV	Kinrossshire	VA	Lanarkshire	XJ	Manchester
SW	Kirkcudbrightshire	VB	Croydon	XK to XP	London
SX	West Lothian	VC	Coventry	XR	London
SY	Midlothian	VD	Lanarkshire	XS	Paisley
T	Devonshire	VE	Cambridgeshire & Isle of Ely	XT to XY	London
TA	Devonshire	VF	Norfolk	Y	Somerset
TB	Lancashire	VG	Norwich	YA	Somerset
TC	Lancashire	VH	Huddersfield	YB	Somerset
TD	Lancashire	VJ	Herefordshire	YC	Somerset
TE	Lancashire	VK	Newcastle upon Tyne	YD	Somerset
TF	Lancashire	VL	Lincoln	YE	London
TG	Glamorganshire	VM	Manchester	YF	London
TH	Carmarthenshire	VN	Yorkshire N.R.	YG	Yorkshire W.R.
TJ	Lancashire	VO	Nottinghamshire	YH	London
TK	Dorset	VP	Birmingham	YJ	Dundee
TL	Kesteven (Lincs.)	VR	Manchester	YK to YP	London
TM	Bedfordshire	VS	Greenock	YR	London
TN	Newcastle upon Tyne	VT	Stoke-on-Trent	YS	Glasgow
TO	Nottingham			YT to YY	London
TP	Portsmouth				

Dates of issue of single & double letter marks (brackets denote reverse issues)

The following list will enable you to establish the year of issue of all double and single letter combinations. (Unfortunately space does not permit the massive listing required to give the triple letter years of issue, although this information is contained in a book compiled by Noel Woodall, "Where's It From, When Was It Issued" and can be purchased through Car Numbers Monthly).

The first date is the original year of issue and so on. When the date is in brackets, this denotes that the number was issued in reverse.

Examples of years of issue:- JN 20 was issued in June 1930. NS 9 was issued in January 1904 and 10 XJ in April 1964.

A	Jan. 1904, May 1905	AZ	Feb. 1928, Nov. 1932 (April 1960)
AA	Dec. 1903, Oct. 1917	B	Jan. 1904 – 1919
AB	Jan. 1904, Aug. 1921	BA	Dec. 1903, June 1931
AC	Dec. 1903, Apr. 1921 (Aug 1958)	BB	Jan. 1904, Jan. 1925 (April 1963)
AD	Dec. 1903, Sept. 1921 (Jan. 1960)	BC	Jan. 1904, Dec. 1924
AE	Jan. 1904, Feb. 1920	BD	Dec. 1903, Sept. 1924
AF	Dec. 1903, Nov. 1924	BE	Dec. 1903, Aug. 1922
AG	Nov. 1925, May 1934	BG	Jan. 1931, Dec. 1947
AH	Jan. 1904, Jan. 1923 (Aug. 1958)	BH	Dec. 1903, March 1923 (Sept. 1962)
AI	Jan. 1904, Dec. 1951	BI	Dec. 1903 (March 1961)
AJ	Dec. 1903, July 1923	BJ	Jan. 1904, May 1925
AK	Dec. 1903, March 1922	BK	Dec. 1903 – 1924
AL	Dec. 1903, March 1922	BL	Jan. 1904, May 1922
AM	Jan. 1904, July 1919	BM	Jan. 1904, Dec. 1920
AN	Jan. 1904, Dec. 1929	BN	Jan. 1904, May 1927
AO	Jan. 1904, April 1924	BO	Jan. 1904, Aug. 1925
AP	Dec. 1903, Feb. 1922 (April 1963)	BP	Jan. 1904, April 1923 (March 1958)
AR	Dec. 1903, Jan. 1921 (Aug. 1959)	BR	Dec. 1903, March 1933
AS	Dec. 1903, Dec. 1964	BS	Dec. 1903, Dec. 1964
AT	Jan. 1904, Jan. 1925 (June 1960)	BT	Dec. 1903, Aug. 1926 (Jan. 1960)
AU	Dec. 1903, April 1924	BU	Dec. 1903, Feb. 1937
AV	Sept. 1926, Jan. 1938	BV	June 1930, Aug. 1939
AW	Dec. 1903, 1921 (May 1962)	BW	Dec. 1903, June 1926
AX	Jan. 1904, March 1927		
AY	Dec. 1903, May 1922		

BX	Dec. 1903, July 1929
BY	Dec. 1903, 1922 (June 1960)
BZ	April 1930, Oct. 1946 (May 1961)
C	Jan. 1904 – 1912
CA	Jan. 1904, Dec. 1934
CB	Jan. 1904, June 1930
CC	Jan. 1904, March 1931
CD	Jan. 1904, July 1925 (March 1960)
CE	Jan. 1904, June 1922
CF	Jan. 1921, July 1930
CG	Nov. 1931, Dec. 1934
CH	Dec. 1903, May 1931
CI	Dec. 1903, July 1960
CJ	Jan. 1904, June 1927
CK	Jan. 1904, Oct. 1928
CL	Jan. 1904, Aug. 1927
CM	Jan. 1904, Jan. 1931
CN	Dec. 1903, Nov. 1946
CO	Jan. 1904, June 1926
CP	Dec. 1903, May 1932
CR	Dec. 1903, Feb. 1925 (Sept. 1959)
CS	May 1934, May 1939
CT	Dec. 1903, Sept. 1928
CU	Jan. 1904, Nov. 1957
CV	May 1929, March 1934
CW	Jan. 1904, March 1930
CX	Dec. 1903, Oct. 1927
CY	Jan. 1904, May 1927
CZ	Nov. 1932, Oct. 1935
D	Dec. 1903, June 1913 (July 1964)
DA	Dec. 1903, June 1925 (May 1959)
DB	Dec. 1903, June 1929
DC	Dec. 1903, Dec. 1929
DD	Sept. 1912. June 1926 (April 1961)
DE	Dec. 1903, July 1934
DF	June 1926, April 1930 (July 1962)
DG	April 1930, Sept. 1934 (Aug. 1063)
DH	Jan. 1904, May 1933 (April 1963)
DI	Dec. 1903, Jan. 1963
DJ	Dec. 1903, Sept. 1947
DK	Dec. 1903, April 1935 (April 1961)
DL	Dec. 1903, Oct. 1935
DM	Dec. 1903, July 1936
DN	Dec. 1903, May 1928 (Jan. 1962)
DO	Dec. 1903, April 1932
DP	Dec. 1903, Sept. 1928 (Feb. 1962)
DR	Jan. 1904, March 1932
DS	Dec. 1903, Dec. 1964
DT	April 1927, April 1938 (March 1958)

DU	Dec. 1903 – 1919 (July 1959)
DV	March 1929, Aug. 1931
DW	Jan. 1904, April 1936 (Feb. 1962)
DX	Jan. 1904, July 1932
DY	Jan. 1904, Jan. 1937
DZ	March 1932, Jan. 1947, (June 1960
E	Jan. 1904, Jan. 1925, April 1953 1000-2500 (June 1958 2501-9999)
EA	Jan. 1904, Dec. 1938
EB	Dec. 1903, Jan. 1933
EC	Dec. 1903, Dec. 1931
ED	Dec. 1903, May 1936 (Oct. 1960)
EE	Jan. 1904, Nov. 1930
EF	Dec. 1903, July 1951
EG	July 1931, Nov. 1949
EH	Jan. 1904, June 1927 (March 1964)
EI	Dec. 1903, Nov. 1959
EJ	Jan. 1904, May 1949
EK	Jan. 1904, April 1934
EL	Dec. 1903, Nov. 1924 (June 1959)
EM	Dec 1903, April 1960
EN	Dec. 1903, Dec. 1949
EO	Jan. 1904, Sept. 1952
EP	Dec. 1903, Nov. 1947
ER	July 1922, Sept. 1928
ES	Dec. 1903, Jan. 1928
ET	Dec. 1903, Oct. 1936 (July 1961)
EU	Dec. 1903, Oct. 1949
EV	March 1931, March 1933 (June 1959)
EW	Dec. 1903, March 1937
EX	Jan. 1904, July 1956
EY	Dec. 1903, Sept. 1951
EZ	Oct. 1935, Oct. 1938 (April 1962)
F	Jan. 1904, March 1915 (Feb. 1957)
FA	Dec. 1903, June 1950
FB	Dec. 1903, July 1932
FC	Jan. 1903, Dec. 1925
FD	Dec. 1903, Oct. 1935 (June 1959)
FE	Jan. 1904, March 1928
FF	Jan. 1904, June 1955
FG	April 1925, Oct. 1934 (Oct. 1962)
FH	Dec. 1903, Feb. 1936 (Jan. 1960)
FI	Dec. 1903, Jan. 1958
FJ	Jan. 1904, Aug. 1934
FK	Dec. 1903, March 1942 (April 1963)
FL	Dec. 1903, July 1931
FM	Jan. 1904, June 1936 (June 1962)
FN	Jan. 1904, March 1929 (Jan. 1962)
FO	Dec. 1903, Sept. 1958
FP	Dec. 1903, Aug 1960

FR	Oct. 1904, April 1929		HT	Feb. 1920, July 1924
FS	April 1931, June 1934 (Jan. 1964)		HU	July 1924, July 1927
FT	Dec. 1903, Feb. 1957		HV	June 1930, July 1938
FU	Aug. 1922, June 1929		HW	July 1927, July 1930
FV	April 1929, Dec. 1937		HX	June 1930, March 1933 (Feb. 1960)
FW	June 1929, Aug. 1937		HY	July 1930, July 1933
FX	Jan. 1904, Jan. 1923		HZ	Feb. 1944, April 1956 (Oct. 1964)
FY	Sept. 1905, Jan. 1927		IA	Dec. 1903, March 1932 (Jan. 1958)
FZ	Oct. 1938, May 1942 (April 1963)		IB	Dec. 1903, Aug. 1947 (April 1962)
G	Dec. 1903 – 1921		IC	Dec. 1903, April 1964
GA	– 1921, Jan. 1922		ID	Jan. 1904, July 1958
GB	Jan. 1922, July 1925		IE	Dec. 1903, March 1959
GC	Dec. 1929, March 1930		IF	Dec. 1903, April 1935
GD	July 1925, March 1928		IH	Dec. 1903, May 1952
GE	March 1928, June 1930		IJ	Dec. 1903, April 1930 (Oct. 1958)
GF	March 1930, May 1930		IK	Dec. 1903, March 1927 (May 1970)
GG	June 1930, Feb. 1933		IL	Jan. 1904, Jan. 1958 (Feb. 1958)
GH	July 1930, Sept. 1930		IM	Dec. 1903, Oct. 1950
GJ	May 1930, July 1930		IN	Dec. 1903, Jan. 1954
GK	Sept. 1930, Jan. 1931		IO	Dec. 1903, June 1953
GL	Aug. 1932, June 1947		IP	Jan. 1904, Feb. 1955
GM	Jan. 1920, Feb. 1959		IR	Dec. 1903, April 1960
GN	Jan. 1931, March 1931		IT	Dec. 1903, May 1972
GO	March 1931, May 1931		IU	Dec. 1903, Nov. 1954 (Sept. 1971)
GP	May 1931, Aug. 1931		IW	Dec. 1903, Jan. 1949 (Sept. 1962)
GR	March 1933, Jan. 1948		IX	Dec. 1903, Jan. 1970
GS	Jan. 1928, Sept. 1941		IY	Dec. 1903, Oct. 1954
GT	Aug. 1931, Dec. 1931		IZ	Dec. 1903, Oct. 1954 (May 1971)
GU	March 1929, May 1929		J	Dec. 1903, Nov. 1922
GV	July 1930, April 1946		JA	June 1929, Jan. 1938
GW	Dec. 1931, March 1932		JB	March 1932, Aug. 1936
GX	March 1932, June 1932		JC	March 1931, April 1949
GY	June 1933, Sept. 1932		JD	Dec. 1929, Jan. 1939
GZ	May 1942, Dec. 1947		JE	Jan. 1933, Aug 1947
H	Dec. 1903, July 1912 (June 1953)		JF	April 1930, Dec. 1935
HA	April 1907, Aug. 1934 (April 1960)		JG	March 1929, Nov. 1937 (Sept. 1963)
HB	April 1908, Aug. 1958		JH	June 1931, Dec. 1934 (March 1960)
HC	April 1911, Sept. 1949		JI	Dec. 1903, Feb. 1944 (April 1961)
HD	April 1913, Nov. 1953		JJ	Nov. 1932, March 1933
HE	April 1913, March 1945 (Sept. 1962)		JK	Dec. 1928, Feb. 1948
HF	April 1913, Oct. 1946		JL	April 1932, Oct. 1945
HG	March 1930, Sept. 1948		JM	Dec. 1931, Nov. 1950
HH	Jan. 1904, March 1938		JN	June 1930, Dec. 1937 (July 1963)
HI	Dec. 1903, Sept. 1954 (Nov. 1971)		JO	June 1930, April 1934
HJ	April 1914, June 1930 (May 1961)		JP	April 1934, Aug. 1952
HK	April 1915, Jan. 1921 (Sept. 1957)		JR	Nov. 1932, July 1939
HL	April 1915, April 1943 (July 1963)		JS	Dec. 1903, Sept. 1952
HM	July 1916, Nov. 1929		JT	Nov. 1933, Oct. 1938
HN	Jan. 1921, June 1934 (March 1960)		JU	Dec. 1931, Nov. 1936
HO	Oct. 1917, Oct. 1922		JV	Nov. 1930, Dec. 1946
HP	1919, 1924 (Feb. 1960)		JW	March 1931, July 1936 (Aug. 1960)
HR	July 1919, Jan. 1924		JX	May 1932, May 1947
HS	Dec. 1903, June 1937		JY	March 1932, Feb. 1937
			JZ	Oct. 1946, Aug. 1954 (Nov. 1963)

K	Dec. 1903, June 1914 (April 1960)	
KA	June 1925, Dec. 1927	
KB	June 1914, March 1920 (Jan. 1961)	
KC	March 1920, June 1925 (Sept. 1961)	
KD	Dec. 1927, March 1930 (June 1962)	
KE	July 1920, June 1922	
KF	March 1930, July 1932 (March 1963)	
KG	Aug. 1931, Feb. 1937	
KH	Jan. 1925, Jan. 1930 (July 1958)	
KI	Jan. 1904, March 1961	
KJ	March 1931, Nov. 1932	
KK	June 1922, April 1924	
KL	May 1924, Sept. 1925	
KM	Sept. 1925, Feb. 1927 (Sept. 1963)	
KN	Aug. 1917, July 1920	
KO	Feb. 1927, May 1928 (Dec. 1963)	
KP	May 1928, Oct. 1929 (March 1964)	
KR	Oct. 1929, March 1931 (May 1964)	
KS	Dec. 1903, April 1947	
KT	Jan. 1913, Aug. 1917	
KU	March 1922, Nov. 1926	
KV	Nov. 1931, July 1934 (May 1963)	
KW	Nov. 1926, March 1931 (April 1963)	
KX	March 1928, March 1933 (April 1963)	
KY	March 1931, May 1935 (April 1964)	
KZ	Jan. 1947, Feb. 1954 (Sept. 1962)	
L	Jan. 1904, Aug. 1921	
LA	April 1910, July 1911	
LB	March 1908, April 1909	
LC	May 1905, Nov. 1906	
LD	May 1909, Oct. 1910	
LE	July 1911, Dec. 1912	
LF	May 1912, Feb. 1913	
LG	Dec. 1928, Nov. 1932 (March 1963)	
LH	Feb. 1913, Aug. 1913	
LI	Dec. 1903, June 1959	
LJ	July 1929, May 1934 (Nov. 1960)	
LK	Aug. 1914, March 1914	
LL	March 1914, July 1914	
LM	July 1914, March 1915	
LN	Nov. 1906, March 1908	
LO	March 1915, Sept. 1915	
LP	Sept. 1915, July 1916	
LR	July 1916, July 1918	
LS	Dec. 1903, March 1964	
LT	July 1918, April 1919	
LU	April 1919, May 1919	
LV	July 1932, Aug. 1934 (Oct. 1963)	
LW	May 1919, July 1919	
LX	July 1919, Sept. 1919	
LY	Sept. 1919, Jan. 1920	
LZ	Jan. 1947, Nov. 1957 (Nov. 1965)	
M	Dec. 1903 – 1920	

MA	– 1920 – 1922	
MB	– 1922 – 1926	
MC	Aug. 1920, Nov. 1921 (Feb. 1962)	
MD	Aug. 1920, Nov. 1921, Feb. 1962	
ME	Nov. 1921, May 1923 (June 1960)	
MF	May 1923, July 1924 (Feb. 1961)	
MG	March 1930, March 1949 (March 1962)	
MH	July 1924, Aug. 1925 (June 1960)	
MI	Jan. 1904, June 1952	
MJ	March 1932, Feb. 1936	
MK	Aug. 1925, Sept. 1926 (Feb. 1960)	
ML	Sept. 1926, Aug. 1927 (Sept. 1961)	
MM	May 1926, Dec. 1929 (Jan. 1961)	
MN	Jan. 1906, March 1935 (May 1959)	
MO	May 1922, May 1927	
MP	Aug. 1927, Aug. 1928 (March 1960)	
MR	Jan. 1924, Jan. 1927	
MS	Dec. 1903, Nov. 1930	
MT	Sept. 1928, June 1929 (Feb. 1961)	
MU	Sept. 1929, Dec. 1934 (April 1962)	
MV	July 1931, June 1933 (March 1960)	
MW	July 1927, Aug. 1931 (Sept. 1961)	
MX	July 1912, Aug. 1917 (Feb. 1962)	
MY	June 1929, March 1933 (Feb. 1961)	
MZ	Dec. 1947, June 1950 (Sept. 1964)	
N	Jan. 1904, Oct. 1913 (June 1959)	
NA	Oct. 1913, May 1919 (Dec. 1959)	
NB	May 1919, Aug. 1920 (May 1960)	
NC	Aug. 1920, March 1923 (Oct. 1960)	
ND	March 1923, March 1925 (May 1961)	
NE	May 1925, Aug. 1926 (Dec. 1961)	
NF	Aug. 1926, Feb. 1928 (June 1962)	
NG	Dec. 1930, May 1935 (March 1959)	
NH	Jan. 1904, June 1930	
NI	Jan. 1904, April 1957	
NK	Jan. 1921, April 1925 (Sept. 1960)	
NL	Jan. 1921, Aug. 1925	
NL	Jan. 1921, Aug 1925	
NM	Dec. 1920, Dec. 1926	
NN	– 1921 – 1925	
NO	Jan. 1921, July 1923 (March 1958)	
NP	Aug. 1921, March 1927	
NR	Jan. 1921, Jan. 1927	
NS	Jan. 1904, June 1964	
NT	– 1921, March 1927 (July 1963)	
NU	March 1923, July 1926 (July 1963)	
NV	March 1931, Oct. 1937	
NW	Oct. 1921, March 1925 (April 1958)	
NX	April 1921, Dec. 1925 (Sept. 1959)	
NY	Aug. 1921, Jan. 1926	
NZ	Jan. 1949, Dec. 1957	
O	Jan. 1904, Feb. 1913	
OA	Feb. 1913, Oct. 1915	

OB	Oct. 1915, May 1919		**RD**	Sept. 1928, June 1937 (March 1964)
OC	May 1933, March 1934		**RE**	Jan. 1921, March 1947 (May 1959)
OD	Aug. 1931, June 1934		**RF**	Dec. 1924, July 1932 (March 1960)
OE	May 1919, May 1920		**RG**	Nov. 1928, Dec. 1938
OF	May 1929, April 1930		**RH**	Jan. 1930, June 1934, (March 1962)
OG	April 1930, April 1931		**RI**	Dec. 1903, April 1921 (Feb. 1970)
OH	Jan. 1904 – 1922 (June 1958)		**RJ**	June 1931, April 1938
OJ	May 1932, May 1933		**RK**	– 1922 – 1927 (July 1961)
OK	Jan. 1922, July 1923		**RL**	Nov. 1924, May 1929
OL	July 1923, Nov. 1924		**RM**	April 1924, Dec. 1933
OM	Nov. 1924, Sept. 1925		**RN**	Oct. 1928, Dec. 1939
ON	Sept. 1925, Aug. 1926		**RO**	April 1925, March 1928 (Feb. 1961
OO	Sept. 1961, April 1962		**RP**	Oct. 1924, March 1931
OP	Aug. 1926, July 1927		**RR**	– 1925 – 1928
OR	Oct. 1922, Jan. 1926		**RS**	Jan. 1904, Nov. 1928
OS	Jan. 1904, July 1955		**RT**	May 1925, Oxt. 1933
OT	Jan. 1926, Nov. 1928		**RU**	Nov. 1924, July 1929 (Aug. 1962)
OU	Nov. 1928, Nov. 1931		**RV**	Feb. 1931, Nov. 1936
OV	April 1931, May 1932		**RW**	1924, 1926, Feb. 1961
OW	April 1931, Aug. 1936		**RX**	May 1927, March 1932
OX	July 1927, July 1928		**RY**	Jan. 1925, April 1930
OY	Dec. 1930, Sept. 1934		**RZ**	Feb. 1954, Jan. 1958 (June 1964)
OZ	June 1950, Jan. 1953 (May 1965)		**S**	Dec. 1902, Nov. 1920
P	Jan, 1904, Nov. 1913		**SA**	Jan. 1904, Sept. 1926
PA	Nov. 1913, Dec. 1919		**SB**	Jan. 1904, May 1954
PB	Aug. 1919, July 1921		**SC**	Oct. 1927, April 1931 (Feb. 1963)
PC	July 1921, July 1923		**SD**	Jan. 1904, Nov. 1925
PD	July 1923, Feb. 1924		**SE**	Jan. 1904, April 1956
PE	Feb. 1924, March 1926 (Oct. 1963)		**SF**	June 1924, Oct. 1927 (Jan. 1962)
PF	March 1926, April 1927 (Aug. 1963)		**SG**	Dec. 1920, June 1924
PG	May 1929, May 1930 (May 1963)		**SH**	Dec. 1903, Oct. 1952
PH	May 1927, May 1928 (April 1963)		**SJ**	Jan. 1904, Dec. 1963
PI	Dec. 1903, Oct. 1932 (Jan 1963)		**SK**	Dec. 1903, Aug. 1963
PJ	Aug. 1931, Oct. 1932 Jan. 1963		**SL**	Dec. 1903, June 1964
PK	May 1928, May 1929 (Oct. 1962)		**SM**	Dec. 1903, June 1933 (April 1959)
PL	May 1930, Aug. 1931 (July 1962)		**SN**	Dec. 1903, Nov. 1946
PM	Feb. 1922, July 1927		**SO**	Dec. 1903, Feb. 1952
PN	July 1927, Sept. 1932		**SP**	Dec. 1903, April 1925 (July 1960)
PO	April 1929, June 1934 (March 1959)		**SR**	Jan. 1904, June 1936 (Aug. 1960)
PP	March 1923, March 1928 (Nov. 1963)		**SS**	Jan. 1904, Nov. 1955
PR	Jan. 1923, Dec. 1927		**ST**	Jan. 1904, Jan. 1939
PS	Jan. 1904, Dec. 1964		**SU**	Jan. 1904, Aug. 1961
PT	Nov. 1922, July 1927 (Aug. 1960)		**SV**	Jan. 1904, Dec. 1963
PU	July 1923, Sept. 1925 (Aug. 1960)		**SW**	Dec. 1903, Dec. 1954
PV	July 1932, Dec. 1949		**SX**	Jan. 1904, Jan. 1956
PW	Jan. 1923, Feb. 1927 (Sept. 1961)		**SY**	Dec. 1903, June 1951
PX	April 1923, April 1929 (Feb. 1960)		**SZ**	Aug. 1954, Sept. 1958 (July 1965)
PY	July 1923, April 1929		**T**	Jan. 1904, Oct. 1920
PZ	Jan. 1953, Aug. 1954 (March 1966)		**TA**	Nov. 1920, May 1924
R	Dec. 1903, March 1923 (Nov. 1962)		**TB**	– 1919 – 1922
RA	July 1926, Nov. 1929 (April 1964)		**TC**	– 1922 – 1924
RB	Nov. 1929, Jan. 1934		**TD**	– 1924, April 1927 (May 1962)
RC	May 1931, April 1947		**TE**	April 1927, Dec. 1929 (Oct. 1962)

TF	Nov. 1929, Nov. 1932 (Feb. 1963)	**VH**	Oct. 1927, Dec. 1936
TG	July 1930, April 1935	**VJ**	June 1927, April 1937
TH	July 1929, March 1938	**VK**	May 1929, Sept. 1933
TI	Jan. 1904, Oct. 1959	**VL**	March 1928, Sept. 1937
TJ	Dec. 1932, May 1935 (May 1963)	**VM**	Feb. 1928, May 1929 (Jan. 1963)
TK	Dec. 1927, Oct. 1933	**VN**	April 1929, Feb. 1937
TL	Sept. 1928, Jan. 1942	**VO**	Oct. 1928, March 1933
TM	Jan. 1927, Feb. 1932	**VP**	July 1928, May 1929 (Aug. 1929)
TN	Jan. 1925, May 1929	**VR**	May 1929, July 1930 (May 1963)
TO	April 1924, May 1929	**VS**	Jan. 1903, Dec. 1959 (March 1963)
TP	April 1924, Feb. 1931	**VU**	July 1930, March 1932 (Nov. 1963)
TR	Feb. 1925, April 1931 (Oct. 1960)	**VV**	June 1930, Feb. 1947
TS	June 1904, June 1932	**VW**	June 1927, May 1929 (March 1960)
TT	June 1924, Oct. 1926	**VX**	May 1929, March 1931 (May 1960)
TU	– 1926, Dec. 1928 (Aug. 1963)	**VY**	May 1928, Aug. 1937 (Jan. 1964)
TV	May 1929, Jan. 1934	**VZ**	April 1956, March 1961 (March 1968)
TW	Sept. 1925, June 1927 (Nov. 1959)	**W**	Jan. 1904, Oct. 1919 (March 1960)
TX	Jan. 1926, July 1930	**WA**	Oct. 1919, April 1924 (Oct. 1960)
TY	Sept. 1925, Oct. 1932	**WB**	April 1924, July 1927 (May 1957)
TZ	Aug. 1934, Oct. 1955 (Jan. 1967)	**WD**	Feb. 1930, June 1935 (April 1961)
U	Jan. 1904, Oct. 1921 (May 1957)	**WE**	July 1927, Dec. 1930 (May 1958)
UA	July 1927, Oct. 1929 (Feb. 1959)	**WF**	Aug. 1926, March 1937 (Jan. 1960)
UB	Oct. 1929, April 1932 (Oct. 1959)	**WG**	Nov. 1930, July 1943
UC	Jan. 1928, March 1928	**WH**	May 1927, April 1938
UD	May 1926, Oct. 1938	**WI**	Dec. 1903, Jan. 1966
UE	Dec. 1925, Feb. 1930 (June 1960)	**WJ**	Dec. 1930, April 1934 (May 1959)
UF	July 1925, May 1933	**WK**	Dec. 1926, April 1929 (Sept. 1961)
UG	Jan. 1932, May 1934 (May 1960)	**WL**	Dec. 1925, June 1930
UH	Aug. 1925, Aug. 1931	**WM**	Jan. 1927, Feb. 1934
UI	Jan. 1904, July 1963 (Aug. 1963)	**WN**	June 1927, June 1936
UJ	April 1932, June 1937	**WO**	March 1927, June 1935
UK	June 1925, March 1931 (Jan. 1962)	**WP**	April 1931, Jan 1936
UL	Jan. 1929, March 1929	**WR**	– 1912, July 1921
UM	Jan. 1925, June 1927 (Feb. 1961)	**WS**	June 1934, July 1936
UN	Dec. 1934, July 1936 (Oct. 1961)	**WT**	July 1923, April 1925
UO	Oct. 1926, March 1929	**WU**	April 1925, Feb. 1927 (Oct. 1959)
UP	July 1927, Dec. 1934 (March 1962)	**WV**	Aug. 1931, Feb. 1936
UR	March 1928, June 1931 (Sept. 1961)	**WW**	Feb. 1927, April 1929 (March 1960)
US	Jan. 1903, Jan. 1935	**WX**	April 1929, March 1932 (Aug. 1960)
UT	Jan 1927, Jan. 1932	**WY**	July 1921, July 1923 (March 1961)
UU	May 1929, June 1929	**WZ**	March 1957, June 1958 (June 1968)
UV	June 1929, Sept. 1929	**X**	Dec. 1903, Jan. 1921
UW	Sept. 1929, Dec. 1929	**XA**	Jan. 1920, April 1926
UX	March 1927, April 1932	**XB**	April 1920, June 1920
UZ	Oct. 1955, March 1957 (Oct. 1967)	**XC**	June 1920, July 1920
V	Jan. 1904, July 1922	**XD**	July 1920, Sept. 1920
VA	July 1922, July 1930	**XE**	Sept. 1920, Jan. 1920
VB	June 1927, Dec. 1930 (July 1962)	**XF**	Jan. 1921, March 1921
VC	May 1929, Nov. 1931 (April 1962)	**XG**	Dec. 1929, June 1948
VD	July 1930, Aug. 1938	**XH**	March 1921, Jan. 1922
VE	Sept. 1928, Feb. 1934	**XI**	1922, Feb. 1928 (June 1959)
VF	Feb. 1927, Dec. 1930 (July 1959)	**XJ**	March, 1932, Sept. 1933 (April 1964)
VG	Aug. 1927, April 1937	**XK**	Jan. 1922, May 1922

XL	Jan. 1922, Sept. 1922
XM	Sept. 1922, Feb 1923
XN	Feb. 1923, May 1923
XO	May 1923, Aug. 1923
XP	Aug. 1923, Jan. 1924
XR	Jan. 1924, April 1924
XS	Jan. 1904, July 1956
XT	April 1924, June 1924
XU	June 1924, Oct. 1924
XV	Oct. 1928, Jan. 1929
XW	Oct. 1924, Feb. 1925
XX	Feb. 1925, April 1925
XY	April 1925, June 1925
XZ	Nov. 1957, April 1962 (March 1969)
Y	Dec. 1903, Feb. 1921
YA	Feb. 1921, Sept. 1924
YB	Sept. 1924, June 1927
YC	June 1927, June 1930
YD	June 1930, July 1934
YE	Jan. 1927, March 1927
YF	March 1927, May 1927
YG	March 1932, March 1935 (July 1961)
YH	May 1927, June 1927
YI	April 1921, March 1927 (Sept. 1970)
YJ	June 1932, Jan. 1948
YK	June 1925, July 1925
YL	July 1925, Nov. 1925
YM	Nov. 1925, March 1926
YN	March 1926, April 1926
YO	April 1926, June 1926
YP	June 1926, Sept. 1926
YR	Sept. 1926, Jan. 1927
YS	Jan. 1935, Sept. 1936
YT	June 1927, Sept. 1927
YU	Sept. 1927, Jan. 1928
YV	March 1928, May 1928
YW	May 1928, July 1928
YX	July 1928, Oct. 1928
YY	Sept. 1932, Nov. 1932
YZ	Dec. 1957, Sept. 1962 (Nov. 1970)
Z	March 1927, Jan. 1940 (Feb. 1971)
ZA	May 1933, March 1937 (June 1971)
ZB	April 1935, April 1949
ZC	March 1937, Jan. 1940 (Oct. 1971)
ZD	Jan. 1940, Jan. 1947 (March 1972)
ZE	Jan. 1940, Feb. 1952 (June 1972)
ZF	Aug. 1946, Dec. 1958
ZH	Jan. 1947, Dec. 1948 (Oct. 1972)
ZI	March 1927, May 1933
ZJ	Jan. 1949, June 1950
ZK	April 1949, May 1953
ZL	July 1950, Feb. 1952

ZM	Oct. 1950, Nov. 1959
ZN	Dec. 1951, Feb. 1962
ZO	Feb. 1952, May 1953
ZP	May 1952, Nov. 1961
ZR	June 1952, May 1961
ZT	May 1953, Dec. 1955
ZU	May 1953, May 1954
ZW	June 1953, April 1963
ZY	Oct. 1954, Jan. 1964
ZZ	Jan. 1926

Glossary of Terms, Abbreviations

Autonumerology – the study of car numbers.

Cherished transfer – the transfer of a registration mark, that is cherished by its owner, from one vehicle to another.

C.N.D.A. – Cherished Numbers Dealers Association.

Donor vehicle – The vehicle from which a number is being transferred.

D.O.E. – Department of Environment.

D.O.T. – Department of Transport.

D.V.L.C. – Driver & Vehicle Licensing Centre. The computerised centre for vehicle licensing etc. at Morriston, Swansea.

L.E.O – London Enforcement Office.

L.T.O. – Local Taxation Office. These offices were used for motor vehicle licensing, before the days of D.V.L.C. They no longer exist.

L.V.L.O. – Local Vehicle Licensing Office. These offices are the link between the public and D.V.L.C.

Log Book – The term used for the old style of registration document for a vehicle. Although many still exist, they have been replaced by the V5, when the vehicle has been taxed through an L.V.L.O.

M.O.T. – A common term for a Ministry of Transport annual vehicle test, and certificate. However, it is now the Department of Transport, but the old term seems likely to survive for a long time to come.

Off The Peg – A term created by L.T.O.'s for the retention of a cherished number.

C.N.D.A. – Cherished Numbers Dealers Association.

Recipient vehicle – The vehicle to which a number is being transferred.

Retention certificate – The document issued when a number is transferred from a donor vehicle but a recipient is not available. The number then had to be transferred from the certificate to the recipient, within a certain period. (At the time of going to press, this facility does not exist).

Reverse issue – Many licensing authorities had used all their issues of numbers, therefore the issue was reversed. Example: when Leicester Borough Council reached ABC 999 in the late thirties, they re-issued the ABC series in reverse, therefore creating 999 ABC. Although most reverse issues were allocated many years after the first series had expired.

R.N.C. – Registration Numbers Club

V5 – The form issued by D.V.L.C., known as a Registration Document. Each vehicle that has been licensed since D.V.L.C., began in the mid-seventies, has been issued with a V5. Some people still refer to it as a "log book".

V10 – The application form to licence a vehicle.

V55 – The application form for first licensing of a vehicle and registration at D.V.L.C.

V62 – The application form for a duplicate or first V5.

Vanity plate – The American term for a cherished number plate.

Year prefix – The year letter coming in front of the registration number. First introduced on 1st August 1983, with the prefix "A".

Year suffix – In 1963/4 Local Authorities introduced a year letter to registration numbers. For example Leicester Borough Council added a "B" suffix in 1964, therefore creating ABC 999B.

Advertisements

148

Index